# MODERN SHOTGUNNING

## The Ultimate Guide to Guns, Loads, and Shooting

Dave Henderson

Skyhorse Publishing

Skyhorse Publishing books may be purchased in bulk at special discounts for sales promotion, corporate gifts, fund-raising, or educational purposes. Special editions can also be created to specifications. For details, contact the Special Sales Department, Skyhorse Publishing, 307 West 36th Street, 11th Floor, New York, NY 10018 or info@skyhorsepublishing.com.

Skyhorse® and Skyhorse Publishing® are registered trademarks of Skyhorse Publishing, Inc.®, a Delaware corporation.

www.skyhorsepublishing.com

10 9 8 7 6 5 4 3 2 1

Library of Congress Cataloging-in-Publication Data is available on file.
ISBN: 978-1-61608-293-2

Printed in China

# Contents

## modern shotgunning

The Thompson Center Encore in its shotgun form claimed this Merriams gobbler in Colorado.

# acknowledgements

Please forgive the blatant name dropping, but the fact that major outdoors personalities like Bryce Towsley, Wayne vanZwoll and Jim Zumbo have done forewords for my books is a source of immense professional pride. The fact that they are my friends provides an even warmer feeling.

Don't think that all this is going to my head, however. I just bought one of my previous books, which sells at $24.95 retail, for $1.99 on eBay. It was brand new. I was the only bidder. If you Google my books, you'll find some listed as being written by "David R. Henderson, Ph.D" or "David H. Henderson." I am, however, neither.

I am "David R. Henderson, Dropout." There is a David R. Henderson, Ph.D who writes books but he's a renowned economist from the west coast, not a journeyman shotgunner. David H. Henderson was, in fact, a retired judge and politician from North Carolina who wrote graceful prose about wonderful hunting dogs and fine shotguns. He found it humorous that people would confuse us and we swapped books a time or two—a bit of commerce where I came out ahead.

I've thus spent much of my adult life apologizing for not being one or the other of those men. But it's really not so bad being me.

This is my fifth book, the fourth on shotgunning. With no formal education or literary training, I've waded through four decades of professional writing with the help of countless editors, including Harris Andrews, whose patience and perseverance sculpted this one into readable form.

Hall of Fame trapshooter Frank Little was a close friend and hunting buddy, and a little of his vast shooting knowledge apparently rubbed off. Reading or hanging around and shooting with the likes of gun writing buddies Towsley, vanZwoll, Nick Sisley, John Weiss, Layne Simpson, Don Zutz, John Taylor and Jon Sundra has helped me more than they'll ever know. Knowledgeable figures like Winchesters' Mike Jordan, Hastings' Bob Rott and guns builders Mark Bansner and Randy Fritz have shown me how and why shotguns and various loads do what they do.

Gil Ash, Steve Schultz and thousands of clay and feathered birds have honed my shooting knowledge, and of course my family—Deb and Dawn—have been there with love and support that makes it all worthwhile.

Thank you all for the opportunity.
—Dave Henderson

Then and now: The author's Browning Auto-5 (left) and his Beretta 391.

*To Debbie, whose love and support makes writing for a living possible; and to our daughter, Dawn, who makes it necessary.*

# foreword

There's an old saying in our industry that there are writers who hunt and hunters who write. Dave Henderson is foremost a hunter. He can find game and he'll hit it. But he's also a hunter with the rare ability to translate his experience and knowledge into words.

I've shared hunting camps with Dave from the Arctic to the Deep South, from the Pacific Northwest to the Rockies, from the Canadian bush to the sub-Arctic tundra. He's fun to have in camp — always smiling, enjoying the moment. And he's sensible enough to be ever thankful for it.

We often room together at hunting seminars, and have logged way too many miles together while traveling on the lecture circuit. As a roommate, I can tell you that he snores; he sometimes talks like you can't hear either, and only drinks good scotch when it's coming from my bottle. But over the years I've come to know and trust Dave as a guy who really knows what he's talking about when it comes to firearms. Particularly shotguns.

Shotguns and I have a checkered history. I've made most of the common mistakes made by shotgun hunters, and probably a few more. I viewed shotguns as a simple device that didn't require much knowledge. I was wrong.

My first shotgun was a J.C. Higgins bolt-action and I didn't know much about proper shot sizes, patterning, and all the other little details that can make you a good shooter.

I remember a turkey hunt with famed humor writer Pat McManus. While he and a couple other people watched, I missed a turkey at 20 yards. Being the hunting editor for one of the biggest outdoor magazines in the country, I was horrified and humiliated, particularly given the audience. Someone suggested I try patterning the gun. I did, and was shocked by how far off point it shot. McManus, who is a good buddy, spared me the embarrassment and hasn't written about the incident. Yet.

Knowledge makes everything seem easier and more enjoyable. If you really want to know about something, it takes study time with a good research source. On the subject of shotgunning, this book is THE source.

In his casual style, Dave skillfully guides you through all aspects of shotgunning. He'll explain gauges, chokes, barrel and action types; choice of proper gun and load; how to pattern and read that pattern. He'll show you wingshooting techniques and explain the importance of gun fit, adjusting your shotgun, dealing with recoil and more advanced subjects like handloading and building your own specialty guns.

I wish I had this book many years ago, but after 50 years of shooting shotguns, I'm mighty glad to have it now. I'm still learning, and Dave is the master teacher. You won't find this book on a shelf in my library. It'll be sitting next to my desk where I can refer to it frequently. This should be a must read for every person who shoots a shotgun, whether he or she is a beginner or a veteran.

Jim Zumbo
Cody, Wyoming
Author, Sports Channel television host

Author Jim Zumbo is not only an expert on hunting but also Dave Henderson's friend.

Old Squaws that fell to an over-under.

# introduction

I can't imagine what my life would have been like without guns. Actually I can imagine it, but don't like the scenario one bit.

Guns, particularly shotguns, have been both a fascination and/or a steady companion for virtually as long as I can remember. More than anything else, they have shaped who I am and what I do. It was with gun in hand that I learned responsibility and respect for property, laws and for life. I learned the meaning of camaraderie and the value of a dollar. Guns taught me the value and necessity of death as it pertains to life.

Shooting guns also taught me many things about velocity, energy, pressure, mechanical functions, distance, the wind, altitude and other invisible forces that far better educated people were left to discover in textbooks.

Paradoxically, guns have also cost me most of my hearing and some close friends. But those losses have been educational too.

Guns have afforded me entry into a world that most folks of this station can view only from the edges. They have been a passport to venues I otherwise could only have dreamed of, and have exposed me to extraordinary people, places and things—and to lasting friendships. Guns have also helped pay the bills for most of my adult life, providing gainful employment when I was qualified for little else.

Dave Henderson values shotguns as hard-working tools.

Without guns in my life, I would possibly own more shirts and jackets without advertising on them; more shoes than boots; and possibly a necktie or two. A life without guns might also have meant a better-paying job, bigger house and newer vehicles—but I would not have been nearly so rich.

All this being said, it may seem odd that I am not a connoisseur of shotguns. I am not the firearms historian or aficionado that many shotgun writers are. I view shotguns as tools and value efficiency, performance and durability over aesthetics, feel and pedigree. There is no passion here for a fancy gun kept in a fancy case—one that can't be used heartily in the field for fear of dents, dings and scratches.

Neither am I a worldly hunter. While I've had the enormous good fortune to hunt in 30 states and 10 Canadian provinces, Africa remains a financial impossibility and folks of my station don't shoot Southern American perdiz, guinea fowl over Tanzanian water holes or driven pheasants over the Scottish moors. Not sure how I would handle someone else toting or loading the gun for me, anyhow.

This is not a history book and it won't cover exotic hunts, high-dollar European guns or the romantic history of firearms. It is instead intended to provide a nuts-and-bolts look at modern shotguns—how to use, evaluate and fix them – and loads, uses and techniques. Admittedly I've spent my adult life getting paid to do things most sensible men would gladly pay to do, and I look forward to sharing that good fortune with you.

When you read this book, we'll be embarking on a personal journey together, and I guess that  means that some personal introduction is in order. You should know that I've never owned a suit, prefer McDonald's coffee to Starbucks', and drive only American vehicles. I am a galloping myopic, deaf as a post—both maladies temporarily corrected—and addicted to caffeine. Any piercings of this body were all accidental and remain unadorned of jewelry.

My watches all have hands and I can't set the clock on the VCR, let alone program the damned thing. Elementary school kids can thrash me at video games, I can't tell you who sings what song on the Top 40 or what shows air what days in prime time.

The AA shooters don't feel intimidated when I arrive at a trapshoot, and despite 40 years of practice, I still sometimes shoot slow when ducks fly fast. I'm a pretty good shot and won some shooting honors but far more have come from writing about it well.

I've attended an opera, a ballet, a Broadway play, the Ice Capades, a piano recital and took a trip to Disney World and don't see any reason to do any of them again. I might go back to the Grand Ole Opry, however, if the opportunity presents itself.

My wife once said—more as a resigned observation than a complaint—that I treat life like a hobby. If that's accurate, Dad should get the credit or blame for that. Afterall, his guns were the initial source of fascination; the spark that ignited all this.

He was neither a gun lover nor a passionate hunter. A combat veteran and a Depression Era kid, he saw guns as tools and killed only for sustenance. He could have simply closed the cabinet door and deflected my pubescent attention when I showed an interest in his guns. But instead, he patiently and diligently taught me what they were and how they worked, all the while impressing the awesome responsibility of their ownership and use.

He was a loving father but I suspect that his basic motive was to keep me from hurting myself or someone else. Although he certainly wouldn't have approved of all the routes his son took, I'm sure that he'd be proud to know that those lessons stuck.

—Dave Henderson
www.HendersonOutdoors.com

# Which Action Is Best for You?

Loosely defined, a shotgun is shoulder-fired ordnance that operates under relatively low chamber pressure to throw short-range loads of pellets or single projectiles (slugs).

Modern shotguns have varied uses, from hunting to shooting games to tactical and home defense. They have come in literally hundreds of forms and sizes, but after 700 years of evolution, they've been boiled down into five basic action types and six bore sizes.

The choice among the various actions and bores is as personal as it is practical. Larger bores put more pellets in the pattern or, larger slugs, and the choice of action is based on weight, intended use, recoil and possibly price point.

## shotgun action

Hunters and shooters have a choice of autoloaders, bolt-actions, pumps, break-actions (single and double barrels) and lever-action in modern shotguns. The latter mention gets an asterisk, as the now-discontinued Winchester 9410 lever-action .410 was the only modern lever-action shotgun ever made.

Actually, there is a sixth type of shotgun, but it's not a different action but loading type—the muzzleloading shotgun.

Each type comes with its own advantages and disadvantages.

The break-open single-shot and side-by-side double barrel were the predominant shotgun designs until the 1930s and 40s with hundreds of small regional manufacturers and individual makers.

Pump and even autoloading repeating designs were patented late in the 19th and early in the 20th centuries, but the break-opens were most common pretty much until World War II.

By that point, two world wars had introduced firearms to a larger segment of the male population. That popularity, combined with the high cost of building labor-intensive double-barrels, sent the industry looking for a less expensive alternative.

The popularity of autoloaders and pumps skyrocketed as the public's interest in double-barrels faded.

*Next page:*
The Franchi I-12 autoloader uses an inertia (recoil) powered action.

The author with an Alabama buck that fell to a 20-gauge Remington 11-87 Sportsman and a Remington BuckHammer slug.

## autoloaders

The autoloader, or semiautomatic, offers the quickest repeating action: firing a round, ejecting the spent hull, and replacing it in the chamber with a loaded one on each trip of the trigger.

These semiautomatics tame recoil better than any other action, using either an inertia block mechanical system or a gas piston to suppress the recoil.

Gas-operated guns generally provide softer recoil but are heavier in weight. The recoil- or inertia-operated guns cycle mechanically and have a tendency be lighter but rougher-shooting.

The drawbacks are that autoloaders are the heaviest shotguns made and the most expensive barring high-end double guns. Autoloaders are also more complicated than other actions, often less reliable (particularly in tough field conditions), and somewhat less accurate in slug-shooting due to the excessive vibration caused by the cycling action.

The John Browning-designed Auto-5, made from 1905 to 1997 (also the Remington Model 11 and Savage Model 720 under the same patent), is considered an American classic autoloader. At least those built in Lieg, Belgium by FN are considered classics. The subsequent Japanese-made A-5s are not held in the same esteem, although they are dependable, durable guns.

Before I got into this business and was exposed all manner of firearms, a Belgian Auto-5 was my gun for all seasons. It had been Dad's gun and came to me when he could no longer hunt in the early 1970s. Despite its fixed full choke it was my bird and small game gun and turned into a deer slayer when loaded with Brenneke slugs.

I added an Invector barrel to take advantage of choke tubes and steel shot, and later a Hastings rifled barrel, and eventually installed a Williams peepsight for deer hunting. Built in 1964, the gun has never malfunctioned, but will kick you all over the lot.

The Remington 1100 is the lightest and oldest gas-operated auto-loading model on the market; it is available in 12-, 20-, 16-, and 28-gauge. Its successor, the 12- and 20-gauge 11-87, features an advanced gas-operated system in a heavier frame and optional 3½-inch chamber (12-gauge) and comes in specialty versions for deer, turkey, and waterfowl hunters.

Remington followed with the short-lived 11-96 Europa, which never overcame design flaws. In 2006 the Model 105 Cti titanium-receiver bottom ejection semi-autoloader was introduced. But once it again, design flaws forced the discontinuation of the model in 2010 when the Versa Max was introduced. The Versa Max is made in Remington's Ilion, New York, plant.

Mossberg dropped its problematic 9200 autoloader early in this century and battled with the design for its 3½-inch chambered 12-gauge successor, the 935, for several years until it was finally introduced in 2004. The 935 Magnum (12-gauge, 3½-inch chamber) and 930 (3-incher) are the only other American-made autoloaders on the market.

Browning's Gold and Silver, Winchester's Super-X2 and –X3 line, Benelli's 12-gauge Super Black Eagle II, M1 and Cordoba, and Beretta's 391 Urika, Optima and Xtrema2 models and the 12-gauge ES100 (formerly the Pintail and a more austere twin of the Benelli Super Black Eagle) are also popular.

Beretta's unique break-action (you've got to see it to understand) UGB autoloader is a high-dollar target gun that attracts curiosity seekers but will have a difficult time finding a market on these shores.

Franchi, Stoeger, Fabarms, BSA and several other European actions are also available on the U.S. market. Weatherby imports a Spanish autoloader and Charles Daly, European American Arms and several other distributors are importing other off-shore designs.

Legacy Sports imports a Turkish-made autoloader marketed under the Escort label. In 2004 Remington broke nearly 200 years of tradition by importing a 12-gauge autoloader made by Baikal in Russia, but quickly discontinued the model in 2008.

For my money, the premier gas-operated autoloader on today's market is the Beretta 391/Urika/Xtrema2/Tekna design. It is the runaway favorite among autoloaders in the sporting clays world with its reliable, soft-recoiling and clean-shooting 391 Sporting design. The 3½-inch Xtrema2, essentially a beefed-up, longer-receiver version of the 391 made for waterfowlers and turkey hunters, has a reputation for durability, reliability and amazingly soft recoil in the field.

As a test, I once shot 50 rounds on a trapfield and 100 rounds on a 5-stand sporting clays course with an older Xtrema and 3½-inch tungsten waterfowl loads. While the design is longer than I'm used to in shooting sports, the recoil was totally acceptable. I've also gone as many as 1,000 rounds between cleaning the gas systems on my sporting 391—an unheard-of exercise with any other gas autoloader I've ever encountered.

Although the 391 Optima remains my personal favorite as a sporting gun, the Benelli Super Black Eagle II is hands-down the best choice as a hunting autoloader.

The gun's ergonomic synthetic stock design, amazing recoil suppression system, backbored barrel and absolutely reliable-under-any-conditions inertia-driven action has supplanted the Ithaca Mag-10 as my waterfowler.

The SBEII is slim, light, and its recoil-operated (non-gas) system will not fail under any conditions and the newest design makes it an absolutely comfortable shooter.

The Remington SP-10 autoloader is the only American-made 10-gauge semiautomatic.

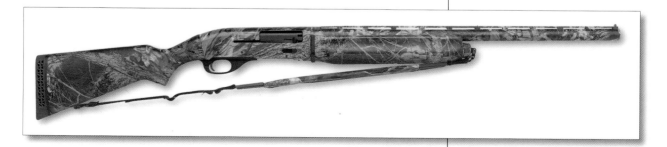

The author's Browning Auto-5 (left) and his Beretta 391.

Fitted with an optional rifled slug barrel, the SBEII is probably the most consistently accurate slug-shooting autoloader on the market. The fact that the barrel extension is actually the top of the receiver, and that both are cryonized, probably helps tame the harmonics that are gremlins to slug-shooting accuracy.

In my experience, the SBEI, 391 Xtrema line and Remington's Versa Max are the only autoloaders that can reliably live up to the claim that they will cycle 2¾-inch, 3-inch and 3½-inch loads equally.

## the pump gun

The pump is the quintessential American action. They've been around since the 1880s (first designed in 1852) and, as mentioned, took over center stage when doubles priced themselves out of the general marketplace and the hunting gun market exploded in the wake of World War II.

A pump features a single barrel over a tubular magazine and the action operates by pulling the forend rearward on a rail to initiate the ejection of the spent hull. Pushing the forend forward again feeds a new shell from the magazine to the chamber and locks the breechbolt back to battery, cocked and ready for the next shot.

The pump-action offers simplicity, durability, low price, and a lighter weight, but you will likely pay for those advantages with heavier recoil.

The compact, lightweight aspect of the pump makes it the darling of the deer stalker, rabbit, turkey and upland bird hunter—and its quick, simple and reliable action attracts waterfowlers who ply their trade in elements that can foul up more sophisticated actions. Those are the same reasons pumps are the first choice for military, law enforcement and tactical applications where reliability is all-important.

Follow-up shots are easier with a pump than with any action other than an autoloader, but again, heavier recoil is the price one pays for the light, compact design.

Classic American pumps include the Winchester Model 12 and exposed-hammer Models 1897 and 97, the Ithaca 37, Remington Models 31 and 870 (with more than 10 million made) and the Mossberg price-point darling Model 500, which sells more than any other shotgun each year.

Remington 12-, 16- and 20-gauge 870s, the 12- and 20-gauge Mossberg 500 and 12-gauge 835 Ultri-Mag and 535 are among the international sales leaders every year. Ithaca Gun Company is back in business after its third failure in 20 years, and the new Ithaca Guns USA M37 is still on dealer shelves in 12-, 16- and 20-gauge specialty configurations for deer hunters, waterfowlers, turkey hunters, small game and bird hunters, and claybird shooters.

Winchester's Speed Pump, based on the old 1300 design, has the fastest and possibly most solid lock-up on the market.

All of the guns just mentioned are made in America, the pump being the only action largely made on these shores today. The Winchester 1300 was a totally American gun, made at the U.S. Repeating Arms facility in New Haven, Connecticut, until that plant was closed early in 2006.

The Browning BPS, a longer version of the bottom-ejection design pioneered by the Remington M17 and Ithaca M37, is available in 10-, 12- and 20-gauge versions with a variety of barrels, including a cantilever rifled slug barrel. It is made for Browning by Miroku of Japan.

Benelli's futuristic Nova, designed out of polymers with the stock and lower receiver one piece, the barrel and upper receiver another, is available in 12- and 20-gauge in smoothbore and rifled-barrel versions. Benellis are made in Italy.

H&R imports a Chinese-made 870 clone under the Pardner Pump label. Charles Daly offers a similar imported pump, Legacy Sports imports a Turkish-made Escort pump (similar to Benelli's Nova plastic stock) and several other European manufacturers feed the American market with small quantities of inexpensive pump-actions.

Virtually all modern pump shotguns, with the notable exception of the short-received Ithaca M37 and Mossberg 500s, are available in 3.5-inch chambered 12-gauge models.

*Above:* Remington 870 is the most popular pump ever made.

*Below:* Legacy Sports imports the Turkish-made Escort pump.

## bolt-actions

The bolt-action is inexpensive, simple, and durable, but cycling the gun is cumbersome to the point of being useless for anything other than deer or turkey hunting, where single shots are the norm.

Today, the bolt-action with a rifled barrel is an excellent slug shooter, even though there are only three models (Savage 220F, 212F and Browning A-Bolt) left on the market.

Once the least expensive, and one of the simplest shotgun actions, the addition of the rifled barrel to the bolt-action models and a few other amenities (like fiber-optic sights, rifle-style synthetic stocks, and scope mounts) has turned the bolt from a beginners' gun into the most inherently accurate slug gun available.

They are still a tough sell, however, as few models remain on the market. Savage, Marlin, Browning the and Mossberg subsidiary of Maverick make the only production bolt-action shotguns today, and only the Savage and Browning models feature rifled barrels.

The Savage 210 was replaced by the greatly improved Model 212 in the Savage product line.

Marlin's Model 55 goose gun, with its 12-gauge, 36-inch barrel, is unique. The Maverick model of the Mossberg line also offers a lower-priced bolt, smoothbore version of the parent firm's 695 rifled barreled slug gun, which was discontinued in 2003.

Marlin's 512 and Browning's supberb but expensive A-Bolt rifled barrel bolt-action slug guns preceded the Mossberg 695 to pasture, but the Browning returned in 2011.

## break-actions: double barrels

"Twice guns" are light and easy to point and carry—classic wingshooting instruments—and are considered the most romantic and personal shotguns.

The over-and-under double is by far the most popular double today, possibly because America is a country of riflemen and the stack-barrel design points like a rifle.

Double guns are used almost exclusively by bird hunters and clay bird shooters, offering an instant choice between two chokes and, in all but the lowest grades, excellent between-the-hands balance.

You won't find many deer hunters shooting doubles with the possible exception of a tradition-bound Old South dog hunter using buckshot (mostly because barrels on double guns usually have different points of aim and a deer gun is aimed rather than pointed as in wingshooting.)

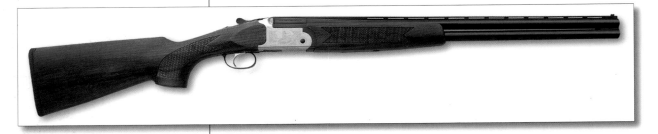

The Ruger Red Label is one of the only over-under production shotguns still made in America.

The most popular version in both side-by-side and over-under doubles is the boxlock, an action devised late in the 19th century that carries the trigger(s), sears, hammers and attendant springs within the action body. The alternative is the sidelock, which carries the sear, hammer, mainspring and tumbler on plates mounted on the sides of the action, inletted into the head of the stock and action bar. The sidelock is a holdover from the days of flintlock and percussion-lock shotguns. The average sidelock had 10 or more individual parts, while the modern boxlock uses just four.

Most modern side-by-sides are boxlocks, which are more bulky but also more durable. High-dollar British guns typically use sidelock actions, which generally offer better trigger pulls and the added safety advantage of interceptor sears.

The drawbacks to doubles are their often gaudy price tags and limited firepower, just one step above the hapless single-shot. Ithaca, Winchester, Fox, Parker and Remington made classic American side-by-side doubles. Ruger tried the American-made Gold Label, bringing it out in 2004 after years of design problems, only to discontinue in 2006.

Weatherby, Kimber, Dakota and Savage offer side-by-sides made for them offshore, while Beretta, BSA, Merkel and a variety of other European and Middle Eastern gunmakers have side-by-sides of their own manufacture.

Small European and Middle Eastern gunmakers who aren't—unlike their American counterparts—burdened by pension plans, workmen's compensation laws, unions, medical plans for employees, OHSA guidelines, etc., are producing good-to-excellent, yet relatively inexpensive (low 4-figures) side-by-sides that are distributed on these shores by a variety of companies.

Perfect examples are the sleek, graceful Turkish doubles made under the American direction for Hatfield Shotguns.

The guns are made by a small but innovative company snuggled in the Taurus Mountains of Southern Turkey and feature high-grade Circassian walnut, 4140 steel receivers, chrome-lined barrels and bone case-hardened finish for about as much as you'd pay for a good auto-loader today.

Originally, I picked up a 28-gauge Hatfield Uplander for my wife. But she now has to borrow it. Go figure.

Out of the box, the gun was graceful if not handsome, but there are lot of siliconed and botoxed beauties out there—how would it perform? Well this one gets a Golden Globe.

Its nimble balance and peak-crowned comb make the 5-pound, 4-ounce Uplander quick and sure to mount and swing. The waist is thin without being delicate and the triggers are crisp. In short, it's a joy in the bird woods and rabbit fields and not too whippy to get an occasional workout on the skeet and 5-stand range at our club.

Old buddy and all-around character Ted Hatfield is a descendant of a Virginia gun-making family and sports a storied personal background that includes (among other things) hunting guide, boat captain, magazine editor, writer, NRA exec, manufacturers brand manager and firearms innovator. He and brother Tim formed Hatfield Classic Shotguns in 2003 after Ted's latest magazine position dissolved.

He helped found Hatfield Rifles and Austin & Halleck muzzleloaders, and the current venture has moved from the utilitarian Uplander to fancy 7-pin sidelock 20-gauges with similar appeal and Turkish backgrounds.

*Top:* Dawn Henderson handles the Turkish-made Hatfield Uplander

*Inset:* Detail of the Uplander 28 from Hatfield Classic Shotguns.

There are plenty of high-dollar European side-by-sides available—just leaf through the advertisements in an issue of "Sporting Classics" or stroll the aisle of the Safari Club International Convention, but they aren't considered hunting guns by anyone of lower station than a sheik or CEO.

Marlin brought back the L.C. Smith, but in name only. The gun currently made under that label is a low-priced Italian double that bears absolutely no resemblance to the classic American design.

Side-by-side prices range from $300 for the Cowboy Action darling Stoeger Coach Gun to $60,000 and more for a high-grade Winchester, Fox or Parker.

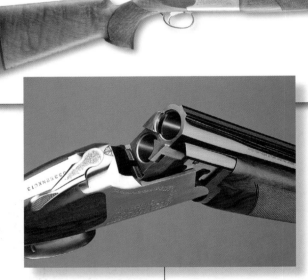

*Above and inset:*
The Browning Citori is one of the most popular over/unders today and is an excellent game or target gun.

## break-actions: over/unders

Browning's Citori line and Beretta's various models are the most popular stack-barrel guns today. But the state-of-the-art is Browning's Cynergy, a unique, low-profile, simple but rugged gun built by Miroku on an American design.

Most over-unders are designed as hunting guns and their hinges and springs simply won't stand up to the constant use required for serious competitive shooters.

The Cynergy's lines go against convention and visually have produced plenty of wrinkled noses since the gun hit dealer shelves in 2004. But its innovative rifle-style trigger and massive monoblock hinge will likely make it a favorite of competitive shooters.

Ruger's Red Label and Ithaca's double are the only over-unders produced on these shores, but there are plenty built offshore that are available through Browning, Winchester, Mossberg, Weatherby, Beretta, Benelli, Franchi, Stoeger, Savage/Stevens, Charles Daly, Fabarms, Kimber and others.

Legacy Sports imports M70 Silma Italian over-unders and less expensive Arthemis Elite Kahn doubles, while BSA imports its own British over/unders.

## break-actions: single-shots

Single-shots are by far the simplest, least expensive shotgun actions—with the exception of those made exclusively for trap-shooting. The basic single-shot also kicks harder than any other gun, and follow-up shots are problematical at best.

Single-shot, break-open guns are built by H&R and New England Firearms, and Thompson Center. H&R and New England Firearms, which are now owned by Marlin, offer entry-level and specialty single-shot guns that range in price from less than $100 in the Tracker version to the $300 12- and 10-gauge turkey models.

The H&R 980 bull-barreled slug gun.

Mossberg's failed SS1 single-shot was dropped in 2003, leaving the TC Encore the only interchangeable barrel design. The latter is actually a modification of a popular pistol design, and probably the most accurate slug shooting shotgun on the market today.

New England Firearms (H&R 1871) makes several low-price Pardner and Topper single-shot guns and bull-barreled 12- and 20-gauge slug guns on the same frames.

There are a variety of break-open single-shot trap guns, ranging from the $400 Stoeger Condor Trap to the $20,000 hand-made Silver Seitz or Ljutic models. Browning's BT-99 (made by Miroku) is probably the most widely used due to its durability, function and relatively affordable (low 4-figures) pricetag.

## lever-action

In the late 1990s Winchester basically chambered its historic Model 94 lever-action rifle as a .410 shotgun—probably because that's the only gauge small enough to fit within the receiver parameters of the narrow, slab-sided lever gun.

The gun was pretty much a plinker, given the limitations of its bore size and action, but had applications for small game. Nevertheless, it was discontinued when the New Haven plant closed in 2006 and was never brought back.

Ithaca once made a lever-action 20-gauge single-shot, but it was phased out even before the first of the company's three business failures in less than 20 years.

The Winchester 9410 lever-action was discontinued in 2006.

## Gauge sizes

### 10 gauge

### 12 gauge

### 16 gauge

### 20 gauge

### 28 gauge

### .410 gauge

# what is "gauge"?

Shotgun bore sizes are delineated by the gauge system rather than calibers. Historically, the term "gauge" refers to the number of equal-sized balls cast from one pound of ordnance lead (lead with a small amount of antimony to harden the mix) that would pass through a hole of specific diameter.

That's one of those definitions that only makes sense if you already know the meaning. To put it simpler, if you mold 12 identical balls from a pound of lead, their diameter will be .729 of a inch, which is 12-gauge. If you mold 20 balls from that pound, the balls will be 20-gauge diameter, and so forth.

The 16-gauge is the classic example since that gauge would accommodate 16 one-ounce lead balls. Shotgun manufacturers still refer to gauges in their models, but they use decimal measurements to identify choke constrictions.

According to the Sporting Arms and Ammunition Manufacturers Institute (SAAMI), the following are nominal interior bore diameters: 10-gauge-0.775 of an inch; 12-gauge-0.729; 16-gauge-0.665; 20-gauge-0.615; 28-gauge-0.550; and .410-gauge-0.410.

Obsolete gauges that remain in SAAMI specifications include the 4-gauge (1.052 inches), 6-gauge (0.919) and 8-gauge (0.835).

Actually, the 8-gauge is still used, but not for hunting or shooting. It's the common gauge for kiln guns, which shoot slugs against silo and kiln walls to clean off clinging material.

Sporting gauges relegated to wallhanger status today are the 24-(0.579), 32-(0.526), and 36-gauge (0.506), largely due to the lack of suitable loads.

The system of expressing shotgun bore sizes by gauge rather than by decimal or metric measurements is, like many things related to smoothbores, a matter of tradition. While five modern gauges are identified by normal measurements, the runt of the litter, the .410-gauge, is the only one labeled by its bore diameter.

That delineation probably comes from the fact that the English numbered gauge system's smallest gauge was 50, which measured 0.453 inch. Presumably, anything smaller needed to be labeled by diameter.

## six modern gauges

The largest, and least used, gauge common today is the 10. Manufacturers originally chambered this gauge for 2⅝-inch shells, but the current chambers are 3½-inches. Today the 10-gauge is a specialty gun used by goose and turkey hunters and those who chase deer with buckshot, all seeking to put as many pellets as possible in their patterns.

When America had hundreds of double-barrel shotgun manufacturers, the 10-gauge was a common waterfowl gun. But after World War II, when hunters went to less expensive single-barrel guns, the heavy 10-gauge essentially went into mothballs.

The Ithaca Mag-10, the world's first 10-gauge autoloader, was introduced by Ithaca Gun in 1974 and took wings the 1980s when it became apparent that steel shot was not going to go away and waterfowlers realized the need for a big bore and more pellets.

A 12-pound heft, lofty price tag and limited application —plus the difficulty of producing consistent patterns with early steel loads and the gun's fixed chokes—kept the Mag-10 from gracing too many gun cabinets. But it was a pioneer.

I had a Mag-10 with a 32-inch barrel. It was dipped in Realtree Advantage livery and Briley fitted it with a screw-in choke tube system. Lengthened forcing cones and a set of Hi-Viz fiber optic sights completed the best goose-taking package I ever toted.

It was a chore to tote in the field, and the ungodly 54-inch length made it a couple clicks past cumbersome in blinds, but once you got it swinging on a flying goose, the damned thing moved like it was on auto pilot.

When Ithaca Gun went bankrupt for the first time in the mid-1980s Remington purchased the rights and tooling to the Mag-10 from the court and the pioneer 10-gauge autoloader was redesigned into the Remington SP-10.

This grouse hunter's 28 gauge over/under may be the perfect shotgun for upland game birds.

The only other 10-gauge autoloader common to the American market is the Japanese-made Browning Gold. The big bore is fairly rare in other actions as well, being chambered only in the Browning BPS pump and H&R (New England Firearms) single-shot.

It was the advent of the 3½-inch 12-gauge that put the demand for 10-gauge in decline. The 12 is the world's most popular gauge since it can handle anything from very light to very heavy loads in 2¾-, 3-, and 3½-inch chambers.

In lighter shotguns, the popularity of the 0.615-inch bore 20-gauge made it a sensible alternative to the heavier, harder-recoiling 12. The in-between 16-gauge was mostly phased out in the 1980s, although Ithaca Gun brought it back early in this century—first in a Model 37 pump field gun and later with a rifled slug barrel—and Remington blew the dust off a couple of old 16-bore models and reintroduced them in 2003. Both moves were largely nostalgic and didn't involve more than a few thousand guns.

## smaller gauges

The 20 is a common choice among upland bird and deer hunters seeking a physically lighter gun to tote on long days afield.

The 20 is one of the four gauges in skeet competition, and with its ⅞- and 1-ounce loads, it is effective on small game. There are 3-inch 20-gauge loads and chambers available, but most aren't conducive to good patterning.

While its primary use was once bird hunting, advances in slug design make the 20-bore an increasingly popular choice among deer hunters.

The 0.550-inch 28-gauge may be the most useful of the small bores because of its comfortable size, soft recoil and effective ¾-ounce payload. While it is also a popular skeet gauge, the 28 is often overlooked in favor of the more powerful 20 in the field. Its primary field use is upland bird hunting since no companies load 28-gauge slugs commercially.

## muzzleloading shotguns

Probably because you can tailor load to specific uses or to the limit of your recoil tolerance, the muzzleloading shotgun has surfaced as a popular alternative to conventional big-bore shotguns in recent years.

Thompson Center, Traditions and CVA—and previously Knight Rifles and now-defunct Austin & Halleck—make 12-gauge, tight-patterning shotguns designed to handle Pyrodex Pellets and 209 primers that are effective on everything from upland birds to turkeys.

Knight's in-line TK2000 features a jug choke in its 26-inch barrel guaranteed to produce 85 percent pattern density in a 30-inch circle at 40 yards—and 97percent at 30 yards. The 7-pound, 9-ounce gun has a 14.5-inch length of pull and comes with a synthetic camo stock and adjustable fiber optic sights.

CVA's blackpowder shotgun is the Optima Pro break-action with a 26-inch barrel built around an internal modified choke. Patterns are adjusted by using CVA cut-adjustable shot cup wads.

Thompson Center's break-action Encore 12-gauge Turkey Gun features a Realtree Hardwoods HD stock and forend, fiber optic sights and a 24-inch barrel with a screw-in, ported choke tube. The specially-built long tube tapers down to a .670 constriction at the muzzle.

The 520 also features a Bold match-grade trigger and short-throw bolt-action that can be adjusted to use percussion or musket caps or 209 shotgun primers for ignition.

The 26-inch Perfect Pattern high vent rib barrel is fitted with a stainless steel Carlson screw-in choke tube. The Black Ice Teflon matte finished barrel is certified for steel shot, lead and heavy alternative loads such as tungsten alloys.

Traditions' break-action Pursuit Pro is available as a 12-gauge muzzleloading shotgun either in matte blued or Realtree Hardwoods Green HD. The guns feature 26-inch barrels with screw-in choke tube systems, or the barrels can be purchased separately to be fitted to the muzzleloading rifle frame.

The Knight TK2000 muzzleloading shotgun uses a 209 shotgun primer for ignition.

U.S. Repeating Arms (Winchester) made a push a few years ago to get their 9410 lever-action .410 exposure as a turkey gun. Certainly you can kill turkeys with any gauge under the right conditions, but if it's a .410 you've got to be virtually within bayonet range. As you'll see later, a .410 pellet hits just as hard as a 10-gauge of the same size. It's just that there are significantly less pellets in a .410 hull.

The .410 is basically a skeet gauge, and is pretty much limited in the field to shooting small game and vermin because of its tiny payload. Most folks think of it as a "kid's" starter gauge, which it can be. But there are plenty of dedicated upland bird hunters, and more than a few dedicated squirrel and rabbit hunters toting the baby bore to take advantage of its light weight and capabilities at short range.

Actually, the gauge system was continued for rifles in gauges up to No. 1 (1.669 inches) until the middle of the 20th Century and is still correct, although rarely used, for smoothbores intended to shoot a single bullet. The system was abandoned when rifle bullets became increasingly elongated, making bore size a less meaningful indication of the weight of the bullet.

### raised ribs
Virtually all pump and autoloading guns are available in versions with a raised rib and at least a single bead sight, or with optional rifle-sighted slug-shooting version. Modern bolt-action and single-shot guns will not feature raised ribs since they are essentially slug or turkey guns that require rifle sights (often fiber optic, for aiming rather than pointing.)

# classic american doubles

Nostalgia sells—and often at outrageous prices. The original A.H. Fox, Winchester, Parker and Ithaca doubles are gone but there are still a few "new" ones out there. We're talking newly manufactured classics.

The snooty world of shotgunning often refers to them as "reproductions," with an inference that they are somehow cheap imitations. In reality, today's "reproductions" are built in America by updated companies to exactly the same specs as the originals. Modern metals, manufacturing method, and finishes actually make them better than the originals.

As of this writing, only Tony Galazan's Connecticut Shotgun Company's A.H. Foxes, Winchester 21s and Parkers are still in production, and Tony is also marketing a round action RBL design of his own.

The company is essentially a custom shop rather than a production arms maker, since each gun is built to individual customer's specifications.

The guns are thus fabulously expensive, all but Galazan's new RBL in the 5-figure retail range, including the $49,000 28-gauge Parker AAHE that Galazan is producing for Remington Arms. They aren't going to be flooding the market, however. Remington previously commissioned Galazan to produce Parkers and the result was three guns sold in a dozen years, the last in 2004.

There were Parker Reproductions (so-named because Remington owns the rights to the original Parker designs and name) being made by a Winchester-owned company in Japan in the 1980s. Last I knew, the Japanese stopped manufacture and the stateside company was in limbo, although it is still listed as part of a New Jersey chemical company that also distributes White Flyer clay targets.

There is also, quite confusingly, a Parker Bros. Makers—the original Parker name—located in the old company's birthplace of Meridan, Connecticut. This company claims the Parker heritage and history but makes modern over/under guns featuring choke tubes and adjustable stocks.

Ithaca Classic Doubles produced high-quality, hand-made versions of Ithaca Gun's classic NID design for several years until it went out of business in 2003, selling its final guns under the Dakota label when Ithaca Gun refused to license the "Classic Doubles" effort any further.

Galazan apparently bought up some of the inventory when ICD closed its doors since he was selling actions, barrels and unfinished stocks for less than $800—which is about what the finished barrel sets cost retail.

The Parker 28-gauge AAHE made for Remington by Connecticut Shotgun Company sells for $49,000.

# All About Barrels

The barrel of this shotgun is fitted with a typical mid-rib fluorescent bead.

A shotgun's barrel is pretty much the soul of the gun. It's the conduit, afterall, that contains and directs shot toward the target—which pretty much describes the essence of shooting.

Any shotgun, regardless of use or action type, is only as good as its barrel; which in turn is judged on the basis of its straightness, rigidity, dimensions, even interior smoothness.

The chamber, at the breech end, is a portion of the barrel that holds the unfired shell in position for detonation. There is a forcing cone immediately forward of the chamber, a span that tapers from chamber diameter down to the actual barrel diameter. Its function is to provide a smooth transition for the ejected wad, shot, and gas from the chamber into the barrel itself.

At the other end, three to seven inches from the muzzle, another forcing cone starts, this one tapering from barrel diameter to choke diameter at the muzzle. One of the functions of the choke constriction is to shape the shot charge before it enters the outside world.

Extending the forcing cones at both ends of the barrel somewhat eases the trauma on the shot charge, giving it more room for the individual pellets to sort themselves out before traversing the tube. This also reduces felt recoil and improves pellet pattern due to the decreased number of deformed pellets.

In older barrels, those made before the advent of plastic, gas-sealing wads, the chamber forcing cones are often short and abrupt—maybe 3/8- to 1/2-inch in length with a 5- to 7-degree taper. Newer designs offer 1.5- to 3-inch forcing cones, which provide a longer and more gentle transition for the shot column.

Backbored, or over-bored, barrels are common on custom turkey and waterfowl guns (although their functionality is often debated), and many target guns and can be found in Benelli, Beretta, Browning Gold and BPS and Winchester Super-X2 12-gauge guns (Invector Plus), as well as in Mossberg's 835 Ultri-Mag, Remington's 1100 Clays and some European guns. A backbored barrel offers a much larger interior diameter, designed to allow an easier passage for the shot charge that results in less pellet deformity, more consistent patterning and less felt recoil.

Backbored 12-gauge barrels commonly sport interior diameters in the 0.735 to 0.740 range, compared to the .729 norm. The term is often used

*Next page:*
Upland game partners — man, dog and gun. Whatever the action, a shotgun is only as good as its barrel.

Staring down the business end. The barrel is the soul of any shotgun.

Remington Hevi-Shot and Hevi-13.

for barrels that have longer forcing cones at the breech and muzzle as well, which serves the same purpose.

I have spent much of my life counting many, many little holes in patterning targets and can't honestly say that I've seen appreciably better performance from backbored barrels than from those with extended forcing cones. In fact, gunmakers tell me that chamber forcing cones longer than 3-inches do not provide any additional benefit.

# modifications

That being the case, however, barrel modifications may be one of the most frequently requested shotgun gunsmithing jobs. But it may also be the least warranted and the most often screwed up—and the alteration of forcing cones heads that list.

Many gunsmiths, probably working from ballistic ignorance, feel that longer is better and may ream cones out to five inches or even more. Ballistic research suggests that there is absolutely no benefit in lengthening a cone to more than 1.5- or 1.75-inches.

Now, you'll never know the length of the forcing cone in a barrel unless you ask customer service at the factory. Most gunsmiths aren't going to know until they measure.

### non-toxic shot fallacy

You may also have heard that lengthening a forcing cone is necessary for better steel shot (or tungsten-iron) performance because those loads have higher chamber pressures and their hardness leads to barrel scoring if the passage of the charge isn't relieved a bit.

Well, it ain't true. First of all, the harder loads don't produce any higher chamber pressures than lead. And even if they did, lengthening the cone would have no effect on that. In fact, lengthening the forcing cone, which requires removing metal from the interior of the barrel, only stands to weaken the barrel at that point, not strengthen it.

The second point is that steel and/or tungsten pellets aren't going to score the barrel simply because in today's thick plastic wads the pellets never touch the barrel walls. They travel from the chamber through the length of the barrel and out of the choke completely enveloped in the plastic tube, the pattern size being determined by the amount of drag the choke constriction puts on the wad (shotcup).

You've undoubtedly heard, and accepted as gospel, the contention that steel or tungsten-iron (and now, Hevi-Shot and the Federal/Winchester variants) shouldn't be shot through older barrels because of those higher pressures and inevitable scoring by the harder pellets.

Many wonderful Winchester Model 12s were retired and Browning

Auto-5 barrels replaced by "savvy" waterfowlers concerned with ruining their favorite barrels (include me in the latter fraternity). But the truth is that it simply isn't a problem.

Granted, in the early days of steel shot when the ammunition manufacturers really didn't know what they were doing, some steel pellets might have been able to escape the shot cups and score barrels. In cases where the bore was radically oversized (backbored), pellets could conceivably slip through slits in the wad and contact the barrel walls. But those problems are largely avoided with today's ultra-efficient shotcups.

The bottom line is that lengthening a forcing cone to 1.5-inches may provide a slight improvement in small-pellet lead patterns; will do nothing for steel or exotic shot patterning and it will take a really practiced hand or imaginative mind to notice any lessening of recoil.

## backboring

Overboring or backboring is essentially extending the forcing cone from the chamber to the choke constriction by opening the barrel diameter several thousandths of an inch beyond the norm.

Again, backboring is touted for waterfowl hunters using steel and exotic shot, for turkey hunters seeking tight, long-range patterns and for buckshot shooters. Truth is, once again, it is a very expensive process that probably doesn't serve any purpose in the aforementioned applications.

Granted, backboring will produce a more uniform pattern for small shot applications like target shooting, and will probably reduce perceived recoil, but it does not help waterfowl, turkey or buckshot patterns—at least not for the reasons you've been told.

If the big or hard-shot patterns are improved by backbored barrels, it's because the increased elbow room in the barrel has compromised the load. Having a bigger tunnel to traverse tends to lessen velocity since the propellant gases aren't as well contained and slip past the charge. A slower charge may pattern better but trading velocity for comfort is commonly seen as bad commerce.

And, as mentioned previously, the larger internal diameter may allow pellets to slip between the wad petals and contact the bore, which means worse patterning with lead loads (more deformed pellets) and possible barrel scoring with hard pellets.

Some shooters want their barrels backbored to a specific diameter because they've been told that it is the magic dimension to decrease recoil or round out patterns. But given the differences in bore diameter and types of steel, barrel to barrel, reaming to specific dimensions may not be feasible.

There are, you see, all manner of internal diameters in guns from the factory, very few right at the nominal 12-gauge specification of .729-inch. The Belgian barrel on my 1960s Browning Auto-5 has a ID of .722, my 2003-vintage Beretta 391 mikes in the .719 neighborhood and I've seen Mossberg 500s in a variety of diameters up to .732.

Generally speaking, non-American shotguns normally have a true bore diameter of approximately 0.005 less than U.S. standard barrels

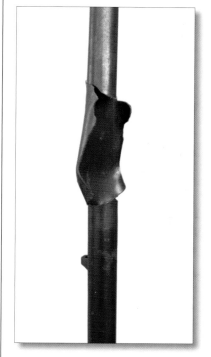

The barrel of this Ithaca Model 37 blew apart when the shot encountered an obstruction blocking the barrel.

(generally a true bore diameter of 0.725), which of course makes a difference when choosing a choke constriction.

Backboring isn't feasible in English barrels, which generally feature a thin and whippy 0.02-inch wall thickness for 2- and 2.5-inch chambers and 0.025 for 2¾-inch guns. American barrels are overbuilt up to 0.035. Belgian, German, French and Italian barrels follow the American logic.

### barrel polishing

A less-expensive, and probably more effective alternative to backboring or the radical lengthening of forcing cones is simply polishing the bore. Polishing merely means removing about .003-inch or less of metal inside the barrel in order to give it a mirror-smooth finish. It can be done to remove pitting or earlier tool marks. Polishing discourages rust and plastic buildup from shotcups and decreased friction when the charge traverses the tube. A good polish job will often increase small-pellet lead patterns by several percentage points.

Chrome-lining barrels achieves approximately the same purpose as a good polishing job, but is much more expensive and makes any future work on the barrel prohibitive. Most gunsmiths won't attempt to ream or install a screw-in choke system in a chrome-lined barrel because the chrome is very hard and may flake out or have to be removed entirely to work on the barrel itself.

### porting

Barrel porting is another very popular barrel modification these days, although the reasoning is dubious. Putting ports or holes in the barrel, usually near the muzzle, is accomplished by either drilling through the barrel walls or etching slots through the walls by electrolysis or a chemical action.

Most folks want their barrels ported because they've heard that it reduces recoil. It actually reduces what is known as "perceived recoil" but the laws of physics make it impossible to reduce the actual rearward momentum of the gun simply by drilling holes in it. A gun of a specific mass will react in a specific manner with calculable force when a specific-sized charge is ignited—and no amount of venting the barrel will reduce that force.

A ported choke tube.

But actual recoil, the rearward thrust of the gun upon ignition of the charge, is in fact only one factor in "perceived recoil," which is what the shooter actually deals with. Other factors include barrel jump and how hard the stock slams your cheek as well as the loudness of the report. How hard your cheek gets slapped can largely be controlled by how the gun fits the shooter.

Thus, the positioning of the ports on the barrel is critical. Cutting them into the sides of the barrel doesn't serve any function. They should be cut in the top of the barrel, as close to the muzzle as possible.

On an over/under double, it doesn't make sense to perforate both barrels. Since porting is done to combat muzzle jump, it really is only effective for the first shot in a 2-shot gun. It's only necessary to port the barrel that will be fired first. It's obviously a slight advantage to operate the top barrel first and port it because holes can be cut in the very top of the upper barrel, better directing down force against barrel jump, whereas the top of the lower barrel is not accessible.

In this day of screw-in choke systems and barrel selectors, you can make that top barrel the choke you want and thus be selected to fire first.

Porting, when done correctly, can and generally does reduce barrel jump significantly. Porting will bleed off gases before they reach the muzzle, which may reduce pressures to the point that a gas-operated semiautomatic will not cycle.

In addition to reducing barrel jump, ports are also known to grab and slow the shotcup, which helps separate it from the shot column. That keeps the shotcup-wad from blowing into the pattern and tends to shorten the shot string for better pattern density.

Porting reduces barrel jump and felt recoil.

While porting a barrel has advantages, the sound pressure wave delivered to the shooter's face and ear is greatly increased by any compensator or porting. Extensive testing has shown that porting increases the report's noise level by at least eight decibels, which may not sound like much, but it represents an increase of 60 percent in the sound pressure magnitude. That's obviously significant.

# barrel length

Who among us hasn't heard of at least one "Long Tom"—usually a long-barreled, single-shot 12-gauge—that was purported to reduce a gallon bucket to door screen at 60 yards. Although it was certainly an exaggeration, at one time the long barrels were more effective to fully burn early smokeless powders and provide magnum velocity and energy.

Today's smokeless powders burn in the few inches of barrel, and the rest of the tube simply orients the charge toward the prospective target.

Granted, longer barrels provide slightly higher velocities, because the expanding gases are confined longer. But that advantage probably ends at about 25 inches. The velocities level off at that point and actually start to drop with extremely long barrels, which apparently act as a brake because of friction after a certain length.

European gunmakers long followed the British dictum that a shotgun's barrel length should be 40 times its bore diameter. That means a 12-gauge gun with with a .729 bore needed a 29.16-inch barrel, 30 inches being a reasonable compromise from a manufacturing prospective.

Americans, on the other hand, cut barrels based on comfort and use. A 26- or 28-inch barrel on a field gun, regardless of action, usually affords sufficient balance and inertia for smooth barrel swinging without being a constant hang-up in brush.

A long barrel offers no ballistic advantage over a shorter one.

Claybird shooters, however, don't worry about brush or carrying the gun and prefer the smooth-swinging characteristics (even at the sacrifice of precise balance) offered by longer barrels. Turkey hunters and slug shooters who aim their guns rather than point-and-swing, are perfectly happy with stubby 20-24 inch barrels that are easier to lug and maneuver through clinging brush.

The move toward shorter barrels was based primarily on marketing—the performance dropped a little and the weight dropped a lot, which made them easier to sell. The long barrels weren't ineffective; they just didn't happen to fit new lifestyles.

A short barrel, even as short at 18 to 20 inches, is actually more effective for slug-shooting because it is stiffer and better resists whip and accuracy-robbing vibration while the relatively slow slug traverses the barrel.

But the long barrel is making a strong comeback today, particularly among sporting clays enthusiasts who see 30-inch barrels as a bare necessity and 32- or 34-inchers as ideal. My trapshooting fortunes improved dramatically when I went from a 28-inch-barreled, personally-cobbled Ithaca pump gun to a buddies' 32-inch Perazzi X8, then 34-inch Browning BT-100 barrels. My personal guns today are 32- and 34-inch BT-99s.

Barrel length is an integral part of wingshooting dynamics. The longer barrel's improved sighting plane is one factor, but probably the biggest is that the inertia involved in swinging a longer barrel makes for a smoother swing and more certain follow-through. It simply improves a shooter's form. Maybe the old-timers had the right idea all along.

Another situation where a long barrel is preferable is in the sport of card shooting. These are the tightest-patterning shotguns in existence, producing ragged one-hole patterns a couple of inches wide. The barrels have no forcing cones and no choke constriction, but are extremely long—often in excess of 60 inches—which allows the shot charge sufficient time to sort itself out and the pellets to get in an orderly line while still in the confines of the tube. In essence, the shot string is formed before it leaves the barrel, resulting in an extremely uniform flight for all the pellets.

# barrel harmonics

Harmonics is the latest consideration in shotguns. The gun vibrates as the ejecta flies down the barrel and the barrel itself whips in reaction to that pressure.

That means that once the barrel temperature reaches a certain point, the gun will shoot to a different point of impact than it did cold. And if one shot is a different velocity than the last—which happens regularly—it exits the muzzle at different point and centers patterns in a different spot. With today's super-tight barrel-choke-load combinations, consistently printing the pattern in the same place is essential.

Understand that the amount of vibration and severity of the whip are fairly constant, shot-to-shot, in a particular gun but ammunition typically isn't. You'll find that slugs and shotshells commonly vary 10-50 fps, shot-to-shot, which means that the projectile or shot charge is leaving the whipping barrel in a slightly different position.

That means, of course, a different point of impact—a wild dispersion when you figure in barrel heat. At the end of a typical 10-shot trapshooting string, pattern placement can shift six inches in some shotguns. With 25 shots, pattern placement can shift up to 12 inches—a 40 percent change.

One way of taming harmonics is to use a heavier barrel, or one of stiffer steel. Ithaca Gun went to the extreme in 2002 with its ill-advised bull-barreled Turkey Slayer II but found that peripatetic turkey hunters don't flock to 10-pound shotguns. Not for $800. I've got one in the vault as a collector's item, and an anchor.

Specialty slug barrels by Hastings and major manufacturers are typically cut from harder, stiffer steel (lower sulfur content) to better withstand the harmonics.

In recent years I've tamed barrel harmonics in my trap, waterfowl and slug guns—as well as some muzzleloaders and rifles by having the barrels, and, in some cases the receivers, cryogenically treated.

Cryogenic tempering—the deep-freezing and deep-reheating of metals—changes the molecular structure, making it harder and stiffer. In many cases it also makes the metal less porous, which aids in subsequent cleaning.

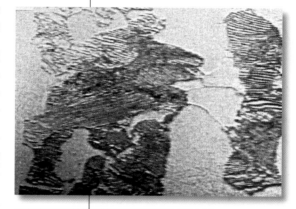
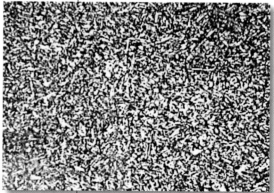

*Above:* A microscopic close-up look at an untreated barrel.
*Below:* A cryogenically treated barrel.

Benelli is the first major manufacturer that I'm aware of that has its shotgun receivers and barrels cryogenically treated. Don't try to drill and tap a Benelli receiver. Cryogenic tempering makes them virtually impenetrable with conventional drills.

Cryogenics have long been used to temper tools, machine parts and cutters and more recently vehicle brakes, race car components, golf clubs, softball bats, tennis rackets and yes, firearms barrels.

All firearms are produced with internal stresses. As the metal is bored, reamed and machined, mechanical stresses are created. As forgings and castings cool, the differing rates of temperature change introduce residual stresses. Even heat treating leaves thermal stresses behind. As mentioned previously, careful manufacturing, of course, provides barrels that shoot well, stresses and all. Cryogenic stress relief, however, can improve even the high-quality barrels by relieving the internal stresses. It's those stresses, or weak spots, that cause barrels to twist and arc as they heat up from firing.

There are several cyrogenic companies out there. I have 300-Below Cryogenic Tempering Services of Decatur, Illinois do my work. They tell me that their process permanently refines the grain structure of a barrel at the molecular level and produces a homogeniously stabilized barrel, whatever that is. They also say that carbon particles precipitate as carbides into a lattice structure and fill the microscopic voids. This creates a denser, smoother surface that reduces friction, heat and wear.

All I know is that it took some guns that had exasperated me and turned them into good shooters. To my way of thinking, cryogenics helps shotgun barrels even more than rifles. Afterall, there is a lot more whip in a shotgun barrel and the shot charge or slug remains in the barrel a lot longer than a bullet does in a rifle, and is therefore more affected by harmonics.

# sub-gauge barrel tubes

Chamber inserts change a gun's gauge in a matter of seconds.

Following the adage that some of us have more guns than we need but none of us have as many as we'd like, the ideal would be to have different shotguns for each of the various uses. Most of us own multiple shotguns, particularly if we shoot competitively and hunt—but another is always handy, and desirable.

A financially and physically comfortable alternative to another gun in the vault is sub-bore barrel tubes, which essentially give you a smaller bore gun in the 12-gauge frame already in your cabinet.

Tubes give you, or a novice that you're bringing to the sport, a big frame (12-gauge) gun scaled down to gentler terms. It gives them the feel and ease of swing of the big gun with significantly less recoil. Small bore chamber inserts or barrel tubes slipped into your goose gun can make it a wonderful, light-recoil yet adequate field gun for quail or doves—a comfortable learning tool for novice shooters who need to learn gun handling and sight picture without the focus-altering anticipation of recoil.

When I slip two Briley Companion 28-gauge tubes into my 12-gauge Ithaca/Fabarms Gamma O/U, the gun weighs the same as it does loaded with two 12-gauge shells. A pair of 28-gauge "minis" inserted in the chamber weigh even less, yet give me the same balance and swing I enjoy with the 12-gauge version.

Granted, there are some tubes on the market that may increase the gun's weight by almost a pound, which to my way of thinking, can defeat the purpose. Briley builds its finned tubes out of titanium and removes weight without weakening the sleeve by making computer designated spiral cuts in strategic spots along the radius. The result is a set of tubes that weigh less than 10 ounces—a savings of more than a quarter pound. And nowhere is excess weight more noticeable than in the muzzle weight of a upland or competitor's scattergun.

The result is a more responsive gun than those using the heavyweight inserts—one that swings into action quicker. That's a plus on the skeet range, sporting clays course or in the field.

I like to shoot several practice rounds with the 28-gauge tubes installed before going into 12-gauge competition or field situation. In addition to the lack of punishment, I find the 28 to be a better teacher, encouraging closer concentration and telling me if I've been "fringing" certain targets with the 12.

Again, you can go ahead and buy a 28-gauge gun. It will be lighter, with a smaller frame, as well as less punishing from a recoil standpoint. But there are there are precious few good ones available for less than four-digit prices and I've effectively added one to my gun vault for less than $500 with a set of Briley tubes. Besides, being slightly over 6-feet tall and a 200-plus pounder for the last three decades, the weight of a 12-gauge frame isn't noticeable, but I've always found smallbore field guns to be too light and whippy in my hammy hands.

And let's face it; there are some things the 12-gauge can do that the 28 can't, so I definitely want both in the same gun case.

The other benefits of the "28-in-12-gauge-package" include greatly reduced recoil (I can add another couple of rounds on a heavy day at the range) and very little loss of effective range on the course or in the field. There isn't a skeet target that can't be broken with a 28, as evidenced by the popularity of small-bore competitions all the way to the national level. And the majority of sporting clays courses are not designed with shots beyond 28-gauge effective range.

And in the field ... Well, a quail or grouse that you can't dump with a 28 has earned its freedom. I frankly don't see a difference between the 12- and 28-gauge in effectiveness at common dove, quail and other upland hunting ranges, with the smaller bore gaining large points for gentleness on frequent-fire outings.

Briley 28-gauge Companion tube slips into a 12-gauge O/U to give the gun a whole new utility.

Fellow writer Bob Robb, a native Californian and inveterate walk-'em-up desert bird hunter, raves about the 28 as a quail gun because "you can carry twice as many shells in your vest"—a true advantage when day-long hikes and plentiful shooting opportunities are de rigueur.

The Benelli SteadyGrip Super Black Eagle II turkey gun.

## special stocks

Tactical shotguns have long been available with pistol grips, but the conventional look was the only choice for sporting guns.

That changed early in the 21st Century when Benelli started offering the SteadyGrip, an angled drop pistol grip similar to that of an AR-15 assault rifle, as an option on its Super Black Eagle and M-1 autoloaders.

In 2004 Remington offered the Boyd's thumbhole laminate stock on its 870 Special Purpose turkey gun, and added a similar option to its 11-87 turkey gun, along with one for the 870 Special Purpose deer gun. Mossberg offered a thumbhole for its 835 pump gun in 2006.

Although the strange grips take a little getting used to, both carrying and mounting, I liked the feel and function of both stocks.

I've used both the SteadyGrip and the Remington Thumbhole for turkeys and took several deer with the thumb-holed 870 deer model. They work well for shooting, both offhand and from a seated position, giving the shooter a stronger draw into the shoulder.

# stocks

If a shotgun is a tool, the stock is its handle—the part with which the shooter makes the most intimate contact. A stock must be sturdy and comfortable and it hurts nothing if it looks good.

Personal comfort and preference will dictate whether the shooter likes the looks and/or feel of a straight grip or pistol-style grip, oiled or glossy finish, even wood, laminate or synthetic construction.

Shotgun stocks have been carved from ivory, cast from metals, molded from polymers, laid up from fiberglass and thin layers of wood. But good old wood is, of course, the most common and successful medium for stock making. All manner of woods have been used: birch, maple, beech, oak, cherry, mahogany and dozens of other domestic and exotic hardwoods that you and I have never heard of. But there is a favorite.

Walnut, in its many forms, reigns supreme as a medium from which to fabricate gunstocks. It is strong, durable, lightweight and flexible. It looks and smells good, is easy to work and takes finishes well. American black walnut is indigenous to the eastern U.S., while Claro walnut, otherwise known as California or Hinds, is found in the West.

Walnut is so popular that you'll also find several varieties of foreign walnut growing on these shores, as well as hybrids. Treasured exotic walnuts include Circassian, Turkish, Persian, Himalayan, Bastogne, English, French and Spanish each with its own distinctive color and tone, grain and feather. But American black walnut is the densest and hardest of all. It is also stiffer and doesn't flex under recoil like European walnut does.

Expensive guns will feature hand-cut and probably elaborate checkering (the higher the grade, the more elaborate) on the grip and forend while an inexpensive gun in any other action usually comes with stamped checkering or none at all.

The shape of the stock is extremely important. An English-style (straight) grip will put the thumb of a shooter used to a pistol grip dangerously close to his nose. A grip that is too thin will tend to dip the shooter's elbow on his grip hand, which actually pulls the barrel in that direction. A palm swell cut, molded or adhered to the grip can correct this phenomenon.

Regardless of how it looks and feels, however, the stock is still a handle. And that handle must fit the shooter or gun is simply a tomato stake.

Author with an Iowa buck taken with a Remington 870 fitted with a Boyds Thumbhole stock.

# All About Chokes

The choke on 19th Century blackpowder hunting guns could be adjusted by simply battering in the muzzle.

*Next page:*
Screw-in chokes provide a versatility to modern shotguns that would have been unimaginable in earlier days.

To put it simply, the amount of choke constriction in your barrel varies with the intended use. A wider spread to the pattern is helpful for short-range shooting like skeet and woodland bird hunting and a denser dispersion of pellets is better for longer shots in open fields and goose blinds.

Because a tighter choke keeps the pellets bunched together at longer range, the load seems to shooter farther. In actuality, the effective range is farther simply because the pellet count stays high farther downrange, but the pellets don't actually fly any farther from a full choke than they do from a skeet choke.

If you center the target, regardless of choke, shotgun loads can be remarkably effective well beyond predictable ranges. I've seen English shooting instructor John Cooley break targets consistently at 80 yards using No. 8 shot and an improved cylinder choke.

He was using a borrowed gun and promo ammunition and claimed that with his gun and premium (magnum shot rather than chilled) ammunition he could regularly break targets at 90-110 yards.

I believe him.

## historically

The advent of smokeless powder shotshells, which made multiple shots quicker, easier, and more feasible, brought about more sophisticated shotgun barrels that were reamed at the muzzle to a specific diameter.

Prior to that, muzzle constriction was achieved by literally battering the muzzle to a smaller diameter, or opened with a mandrel.

Modern shotgunning is virtually ruled by the screw-in choke tube system. While historians will argue over the inventor of choked barrels (first patented in the 1860s), the undisputed Einstein of the screw-in removable choke tube system is Texan Jess Briley.

The Houston machinist developed choke tubes in his garage shop in the mid-1970s, and was smuggling them to live bird shooters in Mexico before they became popular on this side of the border.

Briley's sprawling, automated shop in Houston turns out more than a

million units a year under its label and a host of others, controlling the majority of the market. The Hastings choke shop in Kansas has closed, but Mark Bansner's custom shop in Adamstown, Pennsylvania, still turns out private-label tubes for other companies.

The nominal bore size for a 12-gauge shotgun is 0.729 inches in diameter. It is 0.779 for 10-gauge, 0.667 for 16, 0.617 for 20, and 0.550 for 28-gauge. But the choke constrictions vary slightly in designation between lead and steel (or non-toxic shot). A 12-gauge barrel with no constriction (called cylinder bore) is 0.729. A constriction of 5/1,000 inch (0.724) is considered a skeet choke for lead shooters. Improved cylinder (0.009 constriction or 0.720 diameter) for lead, however, is actually considered a skeet choke for non-toxic loads.

Conventional constriction for a 12-gauge skeet II choke is 0.012 and for modified choke it is 0.019 (or a 0.710 bore diameter). The latter is the same dimension considered improved cylinder for steel shot. Improved modified conventional choke is 0.704 (0.025 constriction), which converts to extra-full for steel shot.

## american choke specifications

| Choke (constriction) | Percentage of pellets in 30-inch circle Yardages | | | | | | | | |
|---|---|---|---|---|---|---|---|---|---|
| | 20 | 25 | 30 | 35 | 40 | 45 | 50 | 55 | 60 |
| Cylinder Bore (.000) | 80% | 69% | 60% | 49% | 40% | 33% | 27% | 22% | 18% |
| Skeet (.005) | 92% | 82% | 72% | 60% | 50% | 47% | 33% | 27% | 22% |
| Imp Cylinder (.011) | 100% | 87% | 77% | 65% | 55% | 46% | 38% | 30% | 25% |
| Modified (.019) | 100% | 94% | 83% | 71% | 60% | 50% | 41% | 33% | 27% |
| Imp Modified (.025) | 100% | 100% | 91% | 77% | 65% | 55% | 46% | 37% | 30% |
| Full (.036) | 100% | 100% | 100% | 84% | 70% | 59% | 49% | 40% | 32% |

Choke tubes of all sizes are cut with threads specific to the gun.

# choke labels are specs

Be advised, however, that all of these measurements are specs, labels. You can buy a choke tube for your gun off the rack at any decent sporting goods store or gun dealer but you may find that it patterns much differently in your Winchester Super-X2 than it does in your dad's Smith & Wesson or your neighbor's Browning BPS, even though it threads into any of them.

All shotgun bores, particularly older ones, vary slightly in internal diameter, which is why a choke tube will pattern differently when screwed into different barrels. The degree of choke in a barrel is simply a measure of constriction from the bore to the muzzle. Since interior barrel dimensions can vary by as much as 20/1,000 of an inch from gun to gun, there is a better way of determining your choke.

Companies that are serious about fitting your gun with choke tubes will need your barrel before they cut tubes.

The true choke size is determined by the difference between the diameter of the bore relative to the diameter of the constriction. By subtracting the diameter of the choke from that of the bore you will be able to determine the amount of constriction (choke) you have regardless of the roll-stamp on the barrel. That measurement is what really counts.

For instance, if you have a choke tube that is cylinder relative to your 0.728 bore, the choke will be modified if used in a barrel of 0.742. But if your barrel's interior diameter measures 0.732 that same choke tube would represent cylinder bore.

For another illustration, let's go back to industry specs. A full choke in conventional terms is 0.694, or a constriction of 0.035, the same dimensions considered to be a modified choke for steel. Extra-full, usually reserved for turkey hunting with lead shot, is 0.040 constriction or a 12-gauge bore diameter of 0.689.

Changing a choke tube.

## constriction

What chokes do is pretty much common knowledge. How they do it, however, is the subject of many different theories.

So how does the microscopic 0.030- to 0.035-inch difference between a truly tight choke and a wide-open boring make such a marked difference in shot dispersion? Well, the difference in diameter in itself simply couldn't make all that difference. The answer is that the choke is just one part of a complex system that affects pattern development.

Granted, choke constriction plays an important role, but just as vital are a pair of dynamic forces that work in concert with the constriction to shape the shot charge before setting it free.

The first factor is the pressure of the trailing wad on the base of the shot charge as it clears the muzzle, and the second is the air resistance (drag) that works against pellets once they escape the controlling wad and powder gases.

The pellets, encased in the plastic shotcup, go from a standing start in the chamber to a 1,200 feet per second (fps) mass in about 0.003 of a second. That puts a lot of pressure and momentum on the wad and pellets. The wad encounters the choke taper, which constricts it slightly from 0.0729 down to 0.695 in a full-choked barrel. That, again, is not much. But the tight choke does pinch down on the wad, slowing it and letting the shot charge escape with little or no pressure from the wad. At the other extreme, a cylinder bore or improved cylinder choke pretty much lets the wad slide through without being bothered, meaning it can remain nestled up against the base of the shot charge. A modified choke gives the wad a slightly tighter squeeze, and improved modified comes down almost as hard as the aforementioned full choke.

Thus, the way choke constriction slows the wad pretty much determines how the shot emerges from the muzzle, at which point it encoun-

Screw-in choke tube systems revolutionized shotgunning.

The rifled choke tube makes it possible for a smoothbore gun to effectively shoot saboted slugs.

ters air resistance. Air works harder against fast-moving objects than against slower ones, and the pellets slow abruptly during the first few feet out of the muzzle.

Pattern and shot string formation depend on how powerful that rear wad pressure is. If it's heavy, as in the case of an improved cylinder choke, the charge is virtually pancaked between the opposing forces of wad pressure and air resistance and the pellets spread outward, widening the pattern. In a full choke the wad is slowed more noticeably. The choke constriction retards the wad, and the pellet string narrows down to squeeze through the smaller opening. Pellets tend to spurt through a full choke because the narrowing is a minor obstruction. They thus escape in a longer line and, since the wad is delayed by the choke taper, the pellets continue on a straighter course because they are not being rammed from behind as in the case of the more open choke.

This phenomenon is more pronounced at high altitudes where air is thinner. Patterns are tighter across the board at high altitudes because of the reduction of the air resistance factor.

In a vacuum, an improved cylinder choke would theoretically deliver 100 percent patterns because of the absence of air resistance. The pellets could travel straight ahead, their superior mass giving them the momentum to outrun the wad and its potentially disruptive impact from behind.

Choke, then, is important only as it retards (or fails to retard) the wad and in how it prepares the shot charge for its impact with air resistance.

# choke systems

As noted, just a few thousands of an inch difference in constriction can, for a variety of reasons, make a huge difference in pattern dispersion. The problem is that most shooting situations require different degrees of constriction. For a long time the only way to overcome the choke problem was to have more than one gun or to have another barrel or several barrels for one gun, which can be an expensive proposition. The average shooter was forced to adapt his shooting to the choke of his gun.

A gun can take on an entirely new personality simply by changing the choke tube.

While virtually all modern shotguns come with a screw-in choke tube system, they are not universal. Manufacturers use different thread patterns and choke tube dimensions. For instance, conventional Winchester, Browning, Ithaca, H&R, NEF, Weatherby, SKB, Savage, Smith & Wesson, Churchill, most Ruger shotguns and Mossberg 500s and 9200s use Win-Choke thread systems, while Remington and 12-gauge Charles Daly autos are threaded for Rem-Choke systems. Beretta, Benelli and Franchi have their own Mobilchoke systems. Browning and Winchester's backbored guns need Invector-Plus choke tube systems, and the Mossberg 835 Ultri-Mag has a system of its own.

## choke versus effective range

| Choke | Ideal Range | Effective Range |
|---|---|---|
| Cylinder Bore | 15-22 yds | 10-27 yds |
| Skeet | 20-27 yds | 15-32 yds |
| Improved Cylinder | 25-32 yds | 20-37 yds |
| Skeet II | 30-37 yds | 25-42 yds |
| Modified | 35-42 yds | 30-47 yds |
| Improved Modified | 40-47 yds | 35-52 yds |
| Full | 45-52 yds | 40-57 yds |
| Extra-Full | 50-57 yds | 45-62 yds |

A choke tube wrench is needed to install this thin-walled tube

## patterning for specific uses

We know that once the shot charge leaves the barrel it spreads to varying degrees, depending on the choke, barrel configuration, distance, type and size of the pellet. The manner in which it spreads is your pattern. And your shotgun's pattern is its signature.

How that particular barrel and choke combination throws a specific load at a specific distance is a dynamic and variable feature unique to that gun. Change chokes or loads and the pattern changes.

While it is essential to know where and how your gun throws a specific load, it is also an ethical imperative if you're hunting. You absolutely must know where that shot charge is going when you trip that trigger.

Knocking a chip of clay target with the fringe of an errant pattern isn't the same as driving a single pellet into the gullet of a bird that will fly off and be lost to die elsewhere.

Patterning techniques vary with the application. In the section of this book devoted to turkey hunting, for example, we outline a technique for patterning turkey loads—extremely full-choked, dense patterns fired from a stationary barrel aimed like a rifle at a standing bird's head and neck.

You don't shoot doves, waterfowl, woodcock or clay birds like that. Wingshooting is a whole different world. You look for consistent, wide but well-distributed patterns at varying distances—sort of a flak screen designed to cut the margin of error when throwing a shot charge at a flying target.

## bigger bore, bigger pattern?

A common misconception among shotgunners is that a larger gauge throws a larger pattern. Afterall, it's easier to score in skeet or trap with a 12-gauge than with a 20, isn't it? Yes, it's easier to break birds with the larger gauge, but not because of the size of the pattern.

The rate of shot spread is controlled by the choke and other factors, not by the bore diameter. Theoretically, the pattern is about the same size whether it's a 12-gauge, 16, 20 or 28. In actual use, you'll probably score higher—and find the pattern marginally wider—with the big

Patterning for gun fit.

bore because there are more pellets in the shot string and more will be be deformed and/or pressured outward, swelling the pattern diameter a bit—not because of a difference in the size of the pattern.

A trapshooter shooting from the 16-yard line, for instance, can count on a 26-inch pattern from a full choke gun at the normal breaking point of 32 yards, and a slightly-larger pattern from a modified barrel, regardless of gauge. At 40 yards the full choke patterns about 40 inches in diameter and a cylinder bore 51 inches, regardless of whether he's shooting a 12-gauge or 28.

## point of impact

Most modern shotguns center their patterns a bit high, usually 4-8 inches above the line of sight at 40 yards. Trap guns are aligned to print 6-12 inches high at that distance because the trap targets are typically shot while rising.

Side-by-side doubles have more flexible barrels and often throw their patterns a bit low. But don't take that as gospel without checking it at the range. Winchester regulated its classic Model 21 to shoot slightly low but in

## effective pattern dimensions *(expressed in inches of diameter)*

|  | 10yds | 20yds | 25yds | 30yds | 40yds |
|---|---|---|---|---|---|
| Spreader Choke | 23 | 37 | 44 | 51 | 66 |
| Cylinder bore | 20 | 32 | 38 | 44 | 57 |
| Improved Cylinder | 15 | 26 | 32 | 38 | 51 |
| Modified | 12 | 20 | 26 | 32 | 46 |
| Full | 9 | 16 | 21 | 26 | 40 |

1960, for reasons that stayed in the board room, changed its mind and moved the point of impact to dead-on.

Over-unders, because the effect of gravity stiffens the barrels that sit one on top of the other, usually shoot slightly higher because of that reduced flex.

## basic patterning

Test your gun on a patterning board. Some folks and clubs use a white-washed or painted steel or iron plate. Lead pellets hitting the surface leave distinctive marks that can be "erased" by rolling another layer of paint over the pattern, ready for the next shot. This type of board should only be used with soft lead shot, however. Steel and other hard shot can ricochet.

Actually, any safe backdrop that will accommodate a 40x40-inch sheet of paper (two strips of wide butcher paper taped together work fine) will do as a patterning board. In fact, this set-up is more useful than the steel plate because pellet counts can be determined away from the range, at a table where comparisons can be made, shot-to-shot.

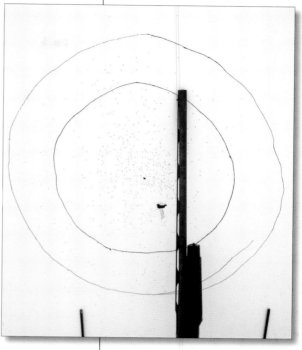

The annular ring produced by this shotgun is a 5-inch donut surrounding the 20-inch core of a pattern.

I like to pattern new guns with an initial shot from a solid rest on a bench at 15 yards to determine if the gun shoots where it's aimed. That only tells me the alignment of the barrel-choke partnership. Follow that with an off-hand shot from the same distance, since the gun will likely shoot to a different point of aim from your shoulder than from the bench. And production guns today, particularly less expensive models, don't always shoot straight, often because the choke tube threads were tapped slightly off center. This can often be remedied by moving the sights or even mounting adjustable optical sights.

Regardless, once you've determined where your gun shoots, examine how it shoots. The industry standard is a target set at 40 yards with a 30-inch circle at the center. The number of pellets your pattern throws within the circle determine the efficiency percentage of your pattern. For example an 80-percent pattern means that eight out of every 10 pellets in that particular load fell within that circle at that distance.

The industry standard pattern percentage for a full choke is 60-70 percent; for modified 55-60 percent and improved cylinder is supposed to put 45 percent of its pellets (in an optimum load) in that 30-inch circle at 40 yards.

You'll find that different load sizes and pellet sizes will pattern differently out of the same choke. It all has to do with the dynamics of barrel and choke, which is discussed elsewhere in this book. When patterning your gun and load, don't base your judgment on one or two shots. You'll need at least 10 shots to get an approximate idea of where and how your gun is patterning.

In fact, when I'm testing various loads, industry experts tell me that it takes at least 100 patterns to get an accurate assessment (more than 95 percent sureity) of a particular gun-load combination. For the field, however, you and I don't need that kind of efficiency—or the shoulder bruising and expense.

There are, believe it or not, scientific methods of thorough pattern reading. I've heard discussed but have never bothered with the Berlin-Wanasse and Thompson-Oberfell methods. I know of only a couple of shooters sufficiently obsessed to utilize such means in patterning their guns. Oh they are good shooters; very good, in fact, but weird people.

# the annular ring

There are far less elaborate ways to determine the efficiency of your pattern. The late Don Zutz used to preach the importance of the "annular ring"—a donut drawn around the core but inside the confines of the 30-inch circle.

First understand that experts look for two different pellet distributions in any pattern—the core or center of the dispersion (usually 20 inches in diameter) and the annular ring, which is a 5-inch wide strip surrounding the core.

Why is the annular ring so important? First, because a shotgun's purpose in wingshooting is to provide a wide hitting area. Even the best shots aren't going to center every target and having sufficient pellets consistently in the annular ring simply expands your margin of error and efficiency.

Not all chokes and loads are efficient at the "useable" fringes of the pattern, even if they throw a dense core pattern. The tendency toward high core density is increased by such things as harder (high-antimony) lead shot that withstands pellet-deforming setback pressures; copper or nickel-plated shot; steel, tungsten and other exotics. This occurs because the sturdier pellets remain round and thus fly straighter to the core of the target. Even open-bored chokes—cylinder bore, skeet and IC—can hammer the core with hard pellets without filling in the annular ring efficiently.

To be efficient, a pattern must spread sufficiently into that annular ring, period.

The industry standard of a 30-inch circle at 40 yards is not always the most practical way to assess a pattern. It's better to determine your average shooting range and test over that distance. A trapshooter, for instance, wants to pattern at 32 to 35 yards for 16-yard events and 40 yards for optimum handicap distances. Skeet shooters are better off patterning at 17 to 20 yards because most shoot their birds before they reach the NSSA distance of 21 yards at midfield. Your average shot at woodcock or quail may be 15 yards; at pheasants 25 yards but a goose hunter may want to know his pattern at 50 yards.

Patterning at your specified distance tells you much more than the 30-inch, 40-yard standard. Shoot at a specified aiming point but don't draw the circles until after the shot. Draw the appropriate circles around the area

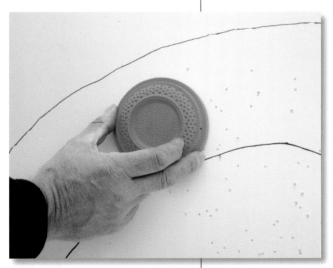

Using a clay to check the effectiveness of the annular ring.

of greatest density. This is done because shotguns are accurate enough to center their patterns in pre-drawn circles.

Again, the point of emphasis is that annular ring. Your goal should be to find the load that puts the most pellets in that annular ring and spreads them most consistently over the area.

How many pellets is enough? Tough to say. But Don's estimation was that three pellets were needed in every area of the target that can be covered with a claybird, since they are about the size of the vital area of most game birds. More is better but three pellets should be sufficient.

Shooting instructor Gil Ash displays target boards that denote the size of shot patterns at various ranges.

# Gun Fit

Instructor Gil Ash discusses the impact point of Phil Bourjailly's pattern and how the gun can be fitted to improve it.

*Next page:*
Ash watches as the gun is mounted and fired at a patterning plate as part of the process of gunfitting.

There are those who would scoff at it. A field grade gun fitted with Grade III replacement walnut, inlaid initials and a smoky case-hardened finish on the otherwise unadorned receiver isn't worth anything. A dressed-up peasant; a waste of time.

To me it simply meant that the gun had obviously been special to someone, and thus well taken care of.

The price was way too high, and the gun far too pretty for my tastes, but the instant I picked up the 1922-vintage 16-gauge Ithaca Flues double from the gun show table, it flew to my shoulder like it was coming home, nestling there comfortably, as content as a dog in an old, worn blanket. I knew it was going home with me.

The chambers had to be lengthened to the modern 2¾ inches and the forcing cones extended, but the old shotgun simply fit me. It shoots where I look. Suffice to say that not all guns do that.

The vast majority of American shooters either select a gun by looks, reputation, price point or opportunity, then "crawl into it," adjusting their shooting style to fit the ordnance. Physical contortions in the placement of the cheek on the stock, and of the front hand on the forend can add or subtract inches to make a gun "fit" the shooter.

For many, it's a trial-and-error process until the shooter finds success; for others, probably more experienced shooters, it may be a subconscious series of moves to the comfort zone.

Regardless of your choice of guns, you are going to shoot it better if you shoot it comfortably. The reason for that is because your dominant eye is the rear sight on a shotgun. How it aligns with the barrel (not necessarily the front bead, which should be ignored when wingshooting) dictates where the gun will shoot.

That positioning must be the same every time for consistent results, and it's a pretty exact technique. An eighth-inch difference in the positioning of your cheek on the stock moves the point of impact more than a foot at 40 yards.

The author's shotgun stock is being heated and bent to prescribed dimensions at the Briley plant in Houston. White objects are ceramic heaters.

But most shooters simply get used to a gun and repetition and the large margin of error afforded by the spreading shot pattern eventually conveys some degree of competency. Only serious shooters, usually competitors or real serious bird hunters, seek to have the gun fitted to them, instead of vice-versa.

Actually, a gun shouldn't be fitted to a shooter until he or she has enough experience shooting to demonstrate a consistent style. It's the same as in my golf club-building business: If the customer averages 110 strokes for a round of golf, I cut them a standard size set of clubs. These folks swing differently every time, and there's no way to build a club to fit them. If, however, they regularly shoot in the low 80s or high 70s, that means they swing more consistently and a club can be built to a specific length, swing speed, swing weight and cast.

It's the same scenario with shotguns. Good fit does make a gun—just like a golf club—far more efficient in the hands of someone who already knows how to use it.

Europeans don't subscribe to the American belief of "crawling into the gun." Overseas they feel that it is imperative that the gun be fit to the shooter before ever going afield.

Understand that in Europe gun ownership is a privilege afforded to small minority of the populace—folks with money who can afford to follow tradition and pay to have guns custom fitted to their physiques. There simply aren't many WalMart Mossbergs in Europe.

# what is gun fit?

Granted, a gun bought off a dealer's shelf is a compromise. It probably fits no one perfectly but can be used casually by virtually anyone, at least someone of average size.

When we're talking gun fit, a tall person theoretically can't shoot the same gun that a short person can. Oh, they can shoot them but we're talking efficiency here—it's going to require a much bigger adjustment by one than the other.

Nor can someone with a round face fit the same gun as a thin-faced person. Women are built differently than men—a fact for which we're all grateful—but that means that their guns must be shaped differently to be effective.

There is a basic means of determining if a particular gun's length of pull is right for you. With your shooting arm extended parallel to the floor, bent upward 90 degrees at the elbow. Place the butt of the gun in the crook of your elbow and see where the tip of the trigger finger lies in relation to the trigger.

It may be just as easy and equally imprecise to see if, when the gun is mounted, the thumb of the trigger hand is sufficiently far from your nose to avoid collision upon recoil.

Shooting instructors and gun fitters denigrate this method because it is so imprecise—but it will tell you immediately if the gun is grossly outsized for you.

Professional fitting, which is the best option if the shooter is serious about wingshooting with a particular gun, will likely be available only at custom shops, wingshooting schools or high-end dealers that have the resources not only to fit but also to tailor the gun to fit you. The customer can expect to pay at least $200 for a fitting, particularly if it entails shooting a "try gun" (adjustable for pitch, length, cast, etc., on the range.) Add another $400 to get it fitted (bend or modify the stock) to your specs.

This articulated "try gun" can be adjusted to fit an individual shooter's characteristics.

I have an Ithaca Gun/Fabarms Gamma over/under that was spawned by a very short-lived partnership between the American and Italian companies in the early 1990s. With 26-inch field barrels, the gun's weight was comfortably situated between my hands and it pointed quickly, but I couldn't seem to shoot it consistently.

Gil Ash watched me shoulder and shoot the gun at a patterning board at his Optimum Shooting Performance School in Houston, Texas. He took some notes and made some calculations. He then sent the gun across town to the Briley Chokes' Lumpkin Road complex where they bent the stock to fit his prescription. The result is a field gun that leaps to the target so naturally that it kills almost without my making the conscious move to the trigger. That's gun fit.

# the factors of gun fit

Critical stock measurements in fitting a gun to a shooter include pull, drop, pitch, and cast. Benelli and Beretta shotguns come with stocks adjustable for all four factors.

On all guns these factors can be determined by simple measurement. The most efficient measuring tool for gun fit that I've encountered is the Shotgun Combo Gauge made by the Robert Louis Company of Connecticut, which does them all.

## length of pull

We'll start with the most common bugaboo, length of pull. Pull is the distance from the front of the trigger shoe (or the front trigger on a double-trigger gun) to the center of the buttstock. Most factory guns come out of the

# patterning for gunfit

Patterning is also useful in gunfitting. In this instance, however, you are not looking at patterning efficiency, but rather where the shot charge centers in relation to a pre-marked aiming point. You can start with a simple test.

The shooter focuses on a marked aiming point, shoulders the gun, and quickly fires. At the Remington shooting school an instructor would then step in front of the shooter, blocking his or her view of the target, and ask the shooter where they thought the pattern would hit.

Gil Ash did the same thing at the American Shooting School in Houston by watching over the shooter's shoulder as he or she mounted and fired the gun at the patterning board.

This eliminated making stock adjustments off a shot that may have been accidentally pulled or triggered before the barrel was precisely aimed at the target. Based on a series of patterns fired correctly, an experienced fitter can then determine the proper stock dimensions for that particular shooter, as Ash did for me.

One technique for verifying fit, or to see if further adjustments are necessary, is to shoot at the pattern board at 15 yards. A trend should emerge from that pattern. Measuring from the center of the aiming point, each inch of displacement translates to a stock adjustment of $1/16$ inch. I'm told that it's a tenet of the Churchill Method.

If the comb of your gun is too high, you will center your pattern too high. If it's too low, your eye is too low and the pattern will obviously be low. A shooter with a pudgy face will generally shoot higher with a particular gun than a thin-faced shooter with the same gun because the mass of the fuller" face puts the eye in a higher position.

Most American guns are neutral in cast, which means they are not bent toward or away from the shooter's face. But again, the shape of the face will effect the direction of the pattern.

If the stock is cast on", which means there is too much wood on the comb (or your face is pudgy) your eye will be out of line with the rib or bead and you are likely to shoot off to the left (for a right-handed shooter; to the right for a lefty). If the stock is cast off" (thin comb or thin-faced) you are likely to compensate in the other direction.

Instructors invariably notice a difference when one of their shooters either loses or gains a significant amount of weight during their instruction, since the point of impact changes dramatically.

It s been said, by a far more eloquent writer than I, that a properly fit and balanced shotgun should follow your wish and swing, without intruding on it.

box at 14- to 14 3/8-inches length of pull. If your sleeve length is 32 inches and you commonly shoot in light clothing, this should be a decent fit.

But not everyone fits that criteria. Youth or ladies models, for example, are often in the 12- to 12½-inch range. If the stock is too short, your gun will shoot high. Also, you'll probably bang your nose with the thumb of your trigger hand, which will make you crawl around for a comfortable spot on the stock.

Conversely, if the pull is too long the gun will shoot low, pose a problem in mounting, and will be a real bear when you're chasing fast crossing targets to your gun side (right for right-handed shooters, left for lefties).

A well-fitted gun will have the pitch adjusted to the shooter, but most of us simply adjust to the length of pull on our specific guns. Creeping the lead hand farther forward on the forend is a method used to artificially lengthen a gun that is slightly short.

So adjusting length of pull is just a matter of lengthening or shortening the stock, right? Yes, but then you've changed the comb (top of the stock where your cheek rests) height, since shotgun stocks typically slope downward toward the butt. And if you remove more than a quarter-inch of length, you're going to need another recoil pad because the old one will be too small to cover the butt.

When cutting a stock, don't use a handsaw. You'll need a high speed table saw to make the cut smooth enough and sufficiently clean around the edges to avoid having to refinish the stock.

A gun can be lengthened by adding spacers or a thicker recoil pad. If you have to add wood, it's a bear to match grain and most likely it will necessitate staining and refinishing the entire stock to hide the differences in grain. It's much, much easier to simply replace the stock with a longer one.

Synthetic stocks are hollow and your alteration options are severely limited, if not non-existent. For instance, since there is nothing in the center of the butt of a synthetic stock to which you can affix the recoil pad, they are fastened by screws to threaded metal inserts in the plastic. Shorten the stock and you've cut off the inserts.

I've seen some attempts at filling the recess in shortened synthetic stocks to give the recoil pad screws purchase, but I'm not convinced that they were worth the effort.

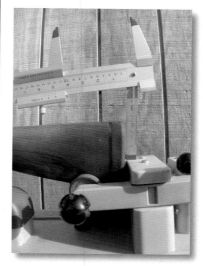

## measuring drop

Factory field guns usually come at 1½-inches of drop comb height, trap guns about 1/8-inch less. Thus, the comb must be adjusted whenever the pull is altered.

You can add lift with a strap-on or stick-on pad or moleskin, and can add cast the same way. Remember 1/16 of an inch moves the point of aim an inch at 15 yards. An eighth of an inch moves it a foot at 40 yards.

Drop is the measurement taken at the topmost surface of a shotgun's stock that determines the elevation of the shooter's head and eye in relation to the bore. To measure drop, a straightedge is laid upon the rib or on top of the barrels and a measurement taken from the bottom of the straightedge to the top of the stock.

Drop at the comb is measured at the very front top of the comb. Drop at the face is an optional measurement taken midway between the front, top surface of the comb, and the heel.

This is the point at which the shooter's face contacts the stock. Because of variations in exact placement, drop at the face is not often thought of as a major factor in gunfitting.

Drop at the heel is measured at the farthest end of the buttstock, where the buttplate or recoil pad meets the top of the comb. It is a vital measurement in determining the placement of the shooter's head and eye on the gunstock.

Get those factors adjusted and you can fine-tune the fit by changing the gun's pitch. Pitch is the angle the stock is cut to meet the shoulder. Normal or

The Shotgun Combo Gauge from Robert Louis Company can measure pitch of the stock, length of pull, and drop at the heel and anywhere else along the comb.

The 1922 Ithaca Flues 16-gauge double fit the author perfectly with no adjustments.

"down" pitch is considered 2 to 2.5 inches.

Pitch governs how the butt lies on the shoulder. Too little pitch will allow the toe of the stock to dig into the shoulder and also has a tendency to allow the stock to slide down and off the shoulder when fired. Too much pitch, on the other hand, makes the stock slip up into the cheek, accentuating felt recoil.

Increasing the down pitch can help heavy men and well-endowed women by making the gun easier to mount and more comfortable. Decreasing the pitch makes it easier to hit fast-rising clay and feathered birds and reduces muzzle jump.

Careful gunfitting includes studying the shape of the individual's shoulder and chest and adjusting the pitch to keep the gun comfortably in position. Women often require more pitch than men.

The most common way of measuring pitch is by standing the gunbutt on the floor with the action or receiver against a squared door frame, then noting the distance (amount of pitch) from the top of the rib to the vertical doorjamb. If the muzzle and barrel are flush to the wall in this position, it's called neutral pitch. If the muzzle touches the wall with the butt squarely on the floor and the receiver is not touching, it's negative pitch. Obviously, negative pitch is very difficult to measure.

The British method of fitting entails also taking measurements from the trigger to the toe, center, and heel of the stock, providing the stocker with precise figures to use for proper adjustment of pitch.

## cast

Older guns, particularly double-barrels, often featured sharply crowned combs, allowing any shooter to easily get his eyes aligned with the beads.

Newer guns, particularly American designs, have much thicker combs topped with a more gradual crown. It can be a chore for some people, particularly those with heavier faces, to get into position. That's where cast comes in.

Cast-off is a lateral bend in a buttstock to compensate for the thickness of the shooter's face. Cast-off is for right-handed shooters, cast-on for lefties. In a bespoke, or custom-stocked, shotgun cast is a part of the stock from the stock's head, where it meets the action, right through the butt.

If there is no cast in the original stock of your gun it can be added by either removing wood from the cheek side of the comb or having the stock bent with heat and a bending jig. Be advised that this is a job for an experienced professional. And they get paid well for that expertise.

Of course we are not all experienced professionals, but then all shooters don't have the means to purchase the services of experienced pros, either. That's why Brownells sells kits that can be installed on existing stocks (with some alteration) so that length of pull, cast, pitch and comb height can be adjusted by mechanical means.

An example of cast in a shotgun stock

A small-framed person needs a smaller gun; one that is as user-friendly as possible. Shooting a gun that doesn't fit the shooter will result in much heavier felt recoil.

Virtually every manufacturer makes a shorter-stocked, thinner-gripped "youth" or even "ladies" model, usually in 20-gauge, with a trigger pull around 12½ inches compared to the standard 14-plus. They feature the same receiver, action and barrel as the conventional-sized versions of the same model, so the smaller stocks can be replaced with a "real" one if the shooter outgrows the smaller version or the gun changes hands.

By the same token, a conventional shotgun can be fitted to smaller-framed shooters with stock and forearm kits from the aftermarket. Outers and other manufacturers offer youth or ladies kits, although most aftermarket kit offerings are typically limited to Remington 870, 1100 and sometimes 11-87s and, in lesser numbers to Winchester 1300s, Mossberg 500s and occasionally the Ithaca M37.

I see it as the ultimate folly to start a novice off with a heavy, big-bore gun and "let them grow into it." When teaching someone to drive you don't put the drivers' seat back too far for them to reach the pedals and steering wheel in hopes that they will "grow into it" and it's just as important that they have a useable system to shoot.

If a gun has a lot of drop in the comb of the stock, the sensation of recoil will be even greater. Fitting squarely into that category are "youth" 20-gauge single-shot guns regrettably chambered for 3-inch loads. They may feel light to carry but that joy takes an immediate turn-around when the trigger is pulled.

The economy-priced, lightweight single-shots are built to sell, not to shoot, and the recoil they mete out can go a long way toward turning off any shooter.

Granted, smaller shooters do need something with less weight to be supported by small arms; something with a shorter stock that keeps the center of gravity to the rear and affords a comfortable reach to the trigger.

But don't think that just cutting off the buttstock will solve everything. For one thing, just sawing off the stock will change the pitch of gun, which could actually accentuate recoil. Be advised the grip and forearm size is as important as stock length when fitting a smaller-statured shooter. A large grip in small hands doesn't allow sufficient thumb-over placement, stretches the hand to reach the trigger and accentuates felt recoil.

Pump shotguns are often chosen as starting guns because they are light, inexpensive, simple and durable. They also kick hard. My daughter, a mechanical engineer, says that it is all explained by Thorson's Restatement of the Second Law of Thermodynamics. In layman's terms Thorson said "you can't get something for nothing."

The physical reaction (backward thrust; see Newton) when a specific load explodes in a chamber always exerts the same amount of energy backward. A heavier gun, however, slows down that reaction and feels like it didn't kick as much.

## balance is important

If a gun fits, you should be able to mount it with your eyes closed and find the rib perfectly aligned—laterally and vertically—when you open them.

A gun that fits is beneficial to trap, skeet and sporting clays shooters and hunting wingshooters but doesn't mean much if you're hunting turkeys, shooting decoying waterfowl or shooting a slug gun.

Balance doesn't mean much in the latter applications, either, but a well-balanced gun is very helpful in wingshooting, where correctly mounting the gun is critical to success.

Ideally, "balanced" means that 50 percent of the gun's weight is between the hands, 25 in buttstock and 25 in barrels. Shotguns for trap-shooting, however, have more weight forward, which tends to steady the hold and accentuate the barrel swing.

Some target guns come with adjustable combs, like this Browning BT-99 trap gun

Some shotguns come with interchangeable spacer kits that can change the pitch and drop of the stock to fit the shooter.

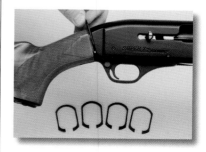

# Recoil and Racket

A good recoil pad, like this Sims Limbsaver, can help reduce felt recoil.

Shotguns kick. Deal with it.

You'll find that it's not just novices and wimps who would like to soften shotgun recoil. Show me a competitive trapshooter today who doesn't extol the virtues of 1-ounce loads over 1⅛ ouncers. Target loads don't kick much, but multiply that kick by 100 or 200 times in a day and, believe me, you'll notice it. Recoil reduction is not simply a matter of avoiding discomfort, it is also an aid in maintaining concentration, which can lead to an improvement in shooting.

That's the reason we're seeing more and more 1-ounce 12-gauge loads on trap and skeet fields and even ⅞-ounce international loads in sporting clays competitors' shellbags. The lighter loads recoil less and may actually pattern better, effectively eliminating the extra pellets that are wasted at the periphery of larger loads' patterns.

Lessen recoil in target or even field loads and you'll be able to practice more and longer—and maybe even look forward to doing it again.

Remington, Federal, Winchester and Lightfield are all offering reduced recoil game and slug loads for that very reason.

Heavy recoil is simply the nature of the beast—an accepted facet of the instrument and the exercise. That's the bad news.

The good news is that the amount of abuse that the shooter has to accept from that beast is controllable. You can lessen recoil by changing loads, going to a smaller gauge or heavier gun or using a gas-operated autoloader instead of a double or pump.

Understand that it's not just physics of the thing—one violent action as a reaction to another. It's the perception affected by the kick, sound and barrel jump the add up to "perceived recoil" which is, afterall, what we're dealing with.

A gunsmith also has several other recoil-lessening options he can offer the potentially shell-shocked customer.

An obvious start is with an aftermarket recoil pad. I'm a big fan of Sims Limbsavers, although research has shown Kick-eez to be the most effective. I have Kick-eez on my trap gun.

Recoil reducers, often referred to as "dead mules" can be placed in stocks or magazine tubes to deaden recoil. You can also reduce the perception by lengthening forcing cones, even backboring barrels—and/or by

*Next page:*
The wing-shaped cutouts in the stock of this Benelli M2 are filled with a high-tech gel that permits the stock to flex under recoil. Part of the ComforTech system, this lessens felt recoil while retaining strength.

# fitting a recoil pad

Fitting recoil pads may seem simple, and it actually is if a few simple steps are followed.

First, if you need to shorten the stock, don't use a carpenter's saw. You can get it done using a very fine-toothed miter saw, sawing with just enough force to cut the wood but not so much that you splinter across the grain. Once you have cut through the side of the stock top to bottom, turn it over and cut from

Components needed to change a recoil pad.

Scribing the recoil pad prior to sanding for fit.

Pad is first sanded while in jig to get a rough fit, then transferred to stock for final sanding.

Sanding recoil pad down to the protective tape.

that side—wood is less likely to splinter if you cut down into it rather than down out of it.

A better choice is to cut the stock with a carbide blade in a radial-arm saw or table saw. Shortening a stock much often changes the pitch, which can only be adjusted back by making another angled cut. Seal the newly exposed wood to keep moisture from seeping into the stock under the new pad.

If you shorten a stock by much more than 1/8 inch, the old screw holes won't orient with the new pad. Sometimes the old heel screw hole will be at a different angle but still useable, but don't expect the toe screw hole to be useful at all.

I've found that putting the stock in a recoil pad jig makes the job handier, although you may want the freedom of holding it in various positions in your hands. B-Square and Miles-Gilbert made good ones.

Use the template from the new pad (or the pad itself) to mark the new hole(s) location. If they are too close to the old ones, drill out the old hole(s) with a quarter-inch drill, cut a plug from a hardware store dowel or simply fill the hole with AcraGlass bedding epoxy, or its equivalent, and let it dry.

Some pads will not have screw holes cut in the surface. Turn them over and insert a punch in the screw hole indent on the inside face and push until it makes a dent on the outside of the pad. Using a soaped (dish washing detergent not oil or grease) razor or Xacto blade, slice down until you contact the punch point. Remove the blade, soap it again and make a similar cut across the first at a 90 degree angle, forming an "X".

Similarly, soap the screw threads and press it through. I like to put a little soap on the screwdriver tip that actually enters the pad material and turn the screws into the stock holes. Once the driver is removed, the screw holes should disappear.

Now the pad must be trimmed. Always buy a pad that is slightly larger than the depth of your stock, taking care because if too much of the perimeter of some high-tech pads is removed, it compromises the effectiveness of the pad.

Now, place three layers of masking tape on the stock finish, flush with the pad and draw a pattern on the top layer of tape. Use a belt or disk sander (glasses, hearing protection, maybe a breathing mask and good light are also necessary) and grind the pad until the pattern disappears on the tape. Now mark the next layer and grind until that disappears; repeat with the third layer, using a very light touch and caution not to nick the stock's finish.

When the sides are thus sanded down, place tape along the heel and toe and grind, blending them to the curve of the sides.

Any fine finish work can be done with an extremely fine file, applied lightly and sparingly.

porting barrels. It's been noted elsewhere in this book that those particular modifications do little to change the physics of actual recoil but they can make the perception softer.

One word of warning here: While porting the barrel reduces barrel jump, which keeps the shooter on the target better and lessens perceived recoil, it also makes the report much louder. If the gun will be used for clay target shooting, where hearing protection is required, porting may be an asset. But if you ported a hunting gun, unprotected ears may convince the shooter that recoil is greater, not less.

Fortunately, shooting at live targets deflects the shooter-hunter's focus away from recoil and the perception is less.

Winchester's Speed Pump lives up to its name as one of the fastest cycling pump shotguns available.

Lubricate the blade with dishwashing detergent when opening a new recoil pad s screw holes

# protect yourself

My daughter was nearly 21 before she and I could have a conversation. It was not the generation difference, or the seemingly natural barrier between parent and growing child.

I simply couldn't hear her.

But hearing aid technology finally advanced to the point, just before her 21st birthday and my 56th, that units could be programmed to help people like me with severe if not profound high frequency hearing loss —the hapless signature of a careless shooter.

I was only 18 when they guy administering the hearing test at the military pre-induction physical pointed out the deficiency pattern and its probable cause. I'd never worn hearing protection while shooting, hunting or working with farm machinery or on vehicles. Nobody I knew ever had.

Oh sure our ears rang for a while after shooting. But it always went away and we could hear just fine again the next day.

Well, hindsight lays bare the fact that believing your hearing comes back fully after severe Tinnitus makes as much sense as leaving the porch light on for Jimmy Hoffa.

In-ear plugs provide sufficient protection against muzzle blast.

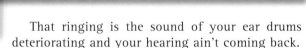

*Right:* Electronic plugs, like these from E.A.R., protect hearing while also amplifying regular tones like conversations or commands. NYX glasses are pellet-proof and come in a variety of lens shades.

*Inset:* E.A.R. electronic plugs can be programmed for the individual shooter's hearing ability.

Hard muffs are the most effective hearing protection but some shooters don't like the bulk, and they cannot be worn with all hats.

That ringing is the sound of your ear drums deteriorating and your hearing ain't coming back.

High frequency hearing loss from muzzle blasts is gradual, incremental and irreversible. At first you lose consonant sounds in conversations, then you can't make out women's voices. Background noise begins to drown out conversations. You eventually feel like you're living in an enclosed booth.

I spent years reading lips, bending my ears outward in movie theaters, Dumbo style, to hear dialogue; guessing certain words or phrases over the telephone.

It's depressing, humiliating. You withdraw from conversations. You become the old guy you used to make fun of.

My hearing at most frequencies was normal for my age, but high frequency hearing was down 70 percent in the left ear, 50-some in the right—classic pattern for a right-handed shooter; right ear being partially closed, and thus protected, by the cheek's contact with the gunstock.

Today I wear hearing protection, and eye protection, whenever I shoot or am near shooting. Although protective glasses don't seem as imperative as hearing protection, I'm also a big believer there after having been hit in the lens countless times by ejected hulls or rebounding scopes.

## damage levels

The consensus among hearing experts is that prolonged exposure to sound levels around 130 decibels can eventually result in damaged hearing. So what is 130 decibels? Well, rifles tested at the U.S. Army Proving Grounds in Aberdeen, Maryland showed decidedly unhealthy sound-pressure levels at 160 to 172.5 decibels.

Short-barreled guns produce exceptionally sharp reports, as do ported barrels, due to the proximity of the blast and/or its direction. A 12-gauge shotgun with a 25-inch barrel produces blast levels in excess of 150 decibels. A short ported barrel might jump that up to 180 decibels.

Earmuffs are the most efficient protection devices available, effectively reducing sound levels to 30-45 decibels. Hardcover muffs reflect sound off their outer shells and also muffle sound inside through dead air space. Several companies, including Walker's Game Ear, market muffs with digital amplifiers built in so that the wearer is protected but isn't cut off from naturally occurring, unobtrusive sounds.

There are plenty of plug-type inserts, from foam to silicone rubber to molded plugs, most of which provide adequate protection if they remain firmly in place while shooting.

In recent years I've been using E.A.R. systems, programmed, molded plugs that fit inside the ear and can be adjusted to allow normal hearing while still protecting against muzzle blast. They are the most comfortable I've tried and feature a unique flexible baffle on the tongue that keeps the plugs firmly seated in the ear.

Take it from one who learned the hard way. Leave the macho image behind when you go to the range or the field. Wear hearing protection and protect your future.

Ear and eye protection are essential for all shooters and people standing nearby.

# Slug Guns

Virtually any shotgun can be used for slug shooting. Some are obviously better than others; others much better.

Doubles, for instance, don't shoot slugs well because the barrels aren't necessarily oriented to the same point of aim. But you will find that break-action single barrels (with the exception of low-priced singles), generally speaking, are the most accurate. Bolt-actions would be next in the out-of-the-box accuracy parade, then pumps and finally autoloaders.

The reason for the difference is vibration. Vibration, both in the receiver and as harmonics in the barrel, is the enemy of accuracy in any firearm. But vibration is most critical in a shotgun.

Consider that a slug gun recoils nearly half an inch before that lumbering slug can find its way out of the muzzle. That's a tremendous amount of barrel movement with it pointing anywhere but where it was originally aimed.

In autoloaders you can also factor in vibration from moving bolts, ejectors and feeding levers—all while the slug is in the barrel—and from the assorted slide rails, forearms, etc. tied to the barrel in pump guns. And perhaps the most telling vibration of all in pumps and autoloaders is that of the barrel shank rattling around inside the receiver. That's the reason bolt-actions and single-shots are inherently more accurate, right out of the box.

On top of that, the vaguerities of big, bulky, slow shotgun slugs in flight only serve to make "accuracy" more problematical. The more you examine the situation, the more amazed you'll be that you ever hit anything with a slug.

On the other hand, you've read about sub-minute-of-angle groups at 100 yards with slug guns. Well, yes, it's been done—by expert shooters with 30-pound custom bench guns, saboted slugs and the right conditions. But that kind of performance is an aberration. It isn't readily repeatable, even by the experts; and it's light years away from what you should expect from an 8-pound hunting gun.

In the everyday world, with commercial ordnance and a weekend shooter, you'll find that anything inside of five inches at 100 yards is asking a lot of an out-of-the-box production slug gun. A slug gun and load that groups inside of 3 inches at 100 yards is a veritable tack driver. Certainly there are more accurate guns and loads, but they are rare and

More than 4 million whitetail hunters use shotguns today.

*Next page:*
Modern slug guns with the correct ammunition and shooter are excellent deer hunting ordnance out to 150 yards.

The Browning Gold Slug Hunter.

require an expert behind the trigger, with the right conditions.

But let's also understand that 100-yard target accuracy isn't essential to the average slug hunter. Most of our shots are well inside of 80 yards at vital areas nearly twice the diameter of a basketball. A difference of an inch or two at 100 yards is moot.

Nevertheless, everyone wants their guns to shoot well. The good news is that virtually any shotgun can be made to shoot more accurately with some experimentation, minor gunsmithing and/or accessories. You can save yourself a lot of headaches when looking for a gunsmith to improve your slug gun if you try someone who works regularly with trapshooters. Trapshooters are looking for many of the same things a slug shooter is —barrel work, taming harmonics, trigger work, reduced recoil, lessening barrel jump, higher combed stocks, etc.

Here are 14 tips for making your slug gun shoot more accurately.

# the barrel

Your first consideration with any slug gun is the barrel. Afterall, that's where the launch is initiated and where everything that affects the direction of flight takes place.

### tip #1: try different choke tubes
If you use your smoothbore barrel for other hunting and shooting, try different choke tubes to see which handles your slugs best. You may find that improved cylinder handles certain slugs better than modified, or vice-versa—and I've seen a few skeet and even full-choked guns that threw rifled slugs very well. You simply must experiment.

Virtually every shotgun manufacturer now offers a rifled choke tube for its guns and there are plenty others on the aftermarket. In my experience, the longer tubes, like Hastings' or Brownings' 5-inchers, offer better accuracy, particularly with sabot slugs.

### tip# 2: aftermarket barrel
While a choke tube will have an effect on how well your gun shoots slugs —and a rifled choke tube will allow you to take advantage of the superior performance of sabot slugs—the best step toward dedicating your shotgun to slug shooting is a fully rifled barrel.

Although a good rifled choke tube may provide accuracy close to that of a rifled barrel at 50-60 yards, it simply can't be expected to spin the slug sufficiently to stabilize it as far as a rifled barrel does. You don't have to be a mechanical engineer to see that it's asking a lot of 2-5 inches of rifling to impart 40,000 rpm spin on a projectile that's already traveling static at peak velocity when it hits the grooves. Obviously it's simply more efficient to spin it from the chamber to the muzzle.

Every major shotgun manufacturer today makes at least one model with a rifled barrel, and also sells the rifled barrels separately. Rifled barrels are typically made of rifle-ordnance steel (much stiffer), which lessens harmonics.

Hastings Barrels is the runaway leader in the aftermarket for rifled barrels and the American Barrel Company began marketing aftermarket barrels for Remingtons, Benellis and Brownings in 2005.

### tip #3: the right ammunition

Don't bother with expensive, high-tech sabot slugs in a conventional smoothbore—the super-expensive sabots are made to be spun by rifling and won't effectively shed their sleeves if they aren't spinning.

You'll probably find better accuracy out of a rifled choke tube if you 're using lower-velocity sabot slugs such as Lightfield Lites or Remington's Managed Recoil BuckHammers or Copper Solids.

### tip #4: pin that barrel

One cure for taming harmonics in a slug gun is pinning or otherwise adhering the barrel to the receiver. Binding the barrel to the receiver with epoxy, shims or pinning it (have a gunsmith put a cap screw through the receiver wall and barrel shank) will take a great deal of the accuracy-destroying vibration out of the system.

Pinning is one move that will make any barrel, smoothbore or rifled,  shoot more accurately. Any barrel that is, other than a bolt-action or single-shot, the designs of which eliminate sloppy barrel-to-receiver fit. Ithaca's Deerslayer II models are the only pumps with free floating barrels affixed permanently to the receiver.

Some guns will improve more than others when the barrel is pinned, depending on how tightly the barrel sleeve fits into the receiver to start with. But, as I said previously, any gun will benefit—I've seen pumps and autoloaders go from throwing "patterns" to tight "groups" with the treatment.

### tip #5: freeze that barrel

Another means of taming harmonics that is becoming popular with shotgunners is cryonizing the barrel. Cryonization is an extreme cold tempering used

*Top:* Range testing a variety of slugs is the only means of detemining the true potential of your slug gun.

*Below:* Pinning the barrel to the receiver with a removable set screw will help the accuracy of virtually any autoloader or pump. This one was done by Dave Klotz, Da-Mar gunsmithing in New York.

on tools, brakes, etc., that hardens and stiffens the metal. It's achieved by freezing the metal at more than 300 degrees below zero, then bringing it back to normal temperatures quickly.

Some Benelli and other high-end shotgun and muzzle-loader barrels are cryonized.

Be advised that if you plan on pinning the barrel, have that work done before having it cyronized. Afterward the receiver will be too hard to drill.

### tip #6: polish the crown

A standard procedure in rifle accurizing is polishing the crown, or the interior lip of the bore where any abnormality will drag on the bullet as it exits. It may not seem as important in a shotgun, but it actually can be. Anything that touches that shotcup, sabot or slug as it exits the muzzle will affect the flight. And you'd be astonished to see imperfections that can come from the factory, particularly if the barrel is button-rifled.

# the trigger

A major factor in consistent shooting for slug guns is the trigger. A shotgun trigger is designed to be slapped, not squeezed like a rifle trigger. And gun companies' liability lawyers like to see substantial creep in triggers that are also set for a hearty slap. The fear is slam-fire on recoil and manufacturers err on the side of caution here.

### tip #7: tighten, lessen pull weight

For a slug gun to shoot accurately you must lighten and stiffen the trigger. Even if your gun is a "buck special" with rifle sights and maybe a rifled barrel, it's going to have the same receiver, internal and trigger mechanism as its counterpart designed for wingshooting with scatter shot.

I don't care if you're the type who can crush cueballs with your fist, nobody can wring full potential out of a firearm with an 8- to 10-pound trigger pull. In a perfect world, we'd have slug guns with crisp 3 to 3.5-pound pulls, but in this world even a 5- or 6-pounder isn't bad so long as there's no creep.

Hastings used to offer a readily adjustable drop-in trigger system for Remington 870s, but the high price kept it from appealing to the masses. More recently Timney Triggers (www.TimneyTriggers.com) has come out with the 870 Trigger Fix kit which allows a reduction in trigger weight down to 2-4 pounds. Remington triggers can actually be honed quite easily. Some triggers can be adjusted more than others—for example, Remingtons, Ithacas, old Savages, Berettas and Benellis are fairly adjustable; Mossberg and Winchester are not.

Some gunsmiths won't want to work on triggers because of liability or the fact that such an adjustment voids the gun's warranty. But anybody who does work for trapshooters can and will do it for you.

## slugs & backbored barrels

Don't try to shoot slugs through a barrel that is backbored (sometimes called overbored). These barrels have over-sized internal dimensions that help them pattern shot better but they are too big for slug shooting, allowing the slug to tilt slightly as it travels down the barrel. Imagine how a tilting slugs reacts when it hits the rifling.

If the barrel is not backbored, however, a rifled choke tube allows you to use the high-tech sabot slugs, which gives you a longer effective range and ballistic efficiency.

# stock work

With a few exceptions, you are going to find that slug guns have shotgun stocks, which are more suited to wingshooting than to sighting through a scope. The choices are much better now than ever before, but if you're shooting a gun that wasn't designed specifically for slug shooting, the stock will need some help.

A lift on the comb of a conventional shotgun stock brings the shooter's eye in-line with a scope.

## tip #8: adjust comb height

The comb must be high enough to allow your eye to look through a scope while maintaining solid contact with your cheek. If you ride higher on the comb, you won't get a consistent look through the glass and the gun will kick you harder.

Mossberg has long offered a unique adjustable comb system on its Model 500 pump. And Remington this year is fitting its 870 Special Purpose Deer and Turkey models with an optional rollover comb thumbhole stock made by Boyds. Bell & Carlson and other aftermarket companies make high-combed or rollover synthetic stocks to fit popular model shotguns.

Actually, any normal shotgun stock can be brought to the correct cheek position with a strap-on Monte Carlo trap pad from Cabela's, a foam version from Beartooth or a stick-on adjustment from Cheek-Eze.

## tip #9: length of pull

Most shotguns are built with a 13.5- to 14-inch length of pull that seems to fit a broad cross-section of shooters. If it doesn't fit perfectly, most of us adjust how we hold the gun to make it fit us. But if you are smaller or larger than "normal," you won't be able to make that gun fit you and shooting it accurately will be difficult if not impossible. It will also kick you harder.

The Benelli Super Black Eagle II fitted with a rifled barrel is an excellent slug shooter.

Women, youngsters and other smaller shooters also have smaller hands, so simply trimming a little length off the stock won't help appreciably. Shorter LOP stocks for youth and ladies' model shotguns are also scaled down through the grip and are therefore much more user-friendly.

Thicker recoil pads and spacers can be added to conventional stocks for larger shooters. Be advised that you may want a shorter length of pull for your slug gun than for your dove gun, since heavier coats and shirts are used in late fall and winter deer seasons.

## different ... twists!

There is a school of thought that faster rifling twist, such as the 1-turn-in-28 inches offered in Browning, Winchester, Beretta, Benelli and Marlin guns, handles high-velocity 12-gauge slugs (1,800 feet per second and faster) better than the conventional 1-34 or 1-35 twist rates.

Tar-Hunt custom slug gun builder and Lightfield load consultant Randy Fritz swears by different twist rates for different slugs. But Hastings Barrel's Bob Rott sees no difference, and all of his Paradox rifled barrels are 1-34.

In fact, my most accurate combination is an Ithaca Deerslayer II with a prototype 1-in-25 barrel and ¾-ounce Federal Barnes Xpander (1,900 feet per second) sabots. But my experience is that internal barrel diameter has a lot more to do with accuracy than rifling twist rate. With any slug gun, you should try a wide variety of suitable ammunition to see which fits your gun best. Even if your buddy has an identical gun, it may shoot the same load differently. SAAMI didn't standardize rifled slug barrel dimensions until the late 1990s, so there is plenty of variety out there.

# dealing with recoil

There are few firearms that kick harder than a shotgun loaded with slugs. The typical 7.5-pound 12-gauge's recoil is roughly equivalent to a .375 magnum rifle or heavier. Anything that makes a slug gun less punishing to shoot will definitely make it easier to shoot accurately.

The laws of physics make recoil an elemental fact—a particular load will exert a specific amount of recoil reaction. It's the same poundage, regardless of gun; but it can be made to feel different. Thus, we are dealing with "felt recoil," and thankfully, there are ways to mitigate that.

As a rule of thumb, heavier guns feel like they kick less than lighter ones; and autoloaders are designed to suppress felt recoil more than pumps, single-shots or bolt-actions.

### tip #10: add recoil reducer

Some Benelli pumps and autoloading models have recoil-suppression devices in the stocks, but they are an exception.

There are a variety of recoil-reduction devices for those shotguns that don't have them built-in. Mercury-filled tubes, often called Dead Mules, that can be inserted in the stock or magazine tube of your shotgun are very effective at suppressing recoil. There are also a variety of specialty recoil pads to add to the effectiveness. Sorbothane models like Kick-Eez are very effective, as are collapsible models like Pachymar Decelerators or the Sims Limbsaver (Remington's R3 is made by Sims) or Hi-Viz pads.

### tip #11: barrel porting

One factor in felt recoil is barrel jump and porting reduces jump while also having the effect of disturbing muzzle gases and allowing sabots to break away freely.

Mossberg has been porting most of its shotgun barrels for several years, and Hastings also offers ported barrels.

Barrel ports must be kept clean, however, since they tend to shave sabot sleeves and collect debris that can effect flight of subsequent slugs.

# sight systems

Slug guns and loads today are short-range ordnance, but their effective range is much longer than 20 years ago. Where a single bead near the muzzle would be sufficient for your father's slug shooting, more is needed today.

### tip #12: fiber optic sights

There are a variety of fiber optic sight systems on the market today, and more and more shotgun manufacturers are offering them on their slug models.

The systems are easy to install; are adjustable, easy to pick up and align and provide relatively precise aiming for use at targets out to 75 yards or so. They are still open sights, however, and require fairly good eyesight. At longer distances they tend to obscure the target and the brightness may darken the areas surrounding a target.

### tip #13: sighting systems

It's gotten to the point where a shooter simply can't aim fine enough with open sights to take full advantage of the longer-range accuracy potential of today's rifled barrels and sabot slugs.

Most optics manufacturers make a compact, long eye relief scope especially for shotguns today. Variables can range from 1.5x to 5x with some larger-objective scopes 2-7x. Fixed scopes

A Benelli Nova with open sights.

2x to 6x are also handy, if the parallax is adjusted at 100 yards or less. Illuminated dot scopes are also popular for quick-point slug shooting.

The right optics will make any slug gun shoot more accurately. Inexpensive rifle scopes aren't likely to stand up to the savage recoil of a slug gun. It takes a scope tested to withstand recoil upwards of a .375 magnum to handle the rigors of a slug gun. Use steel rings rather than aluminum to handle that concussion.

Scope rails may be mounted directly on receivers like the Remington 870 or Ithaca 37/87. But cantilever barrels or saddle-style mounts are necessary on many since the receiver steel isn't thick enough to give mounting screw sufficient purchase.

# to clean or not to clean

Depending on what type of barrel you use, cleaning or not cleaning it can make a difference in accuracy.

### tip #14: when to clean

Believe it or not, many smoothbore slug barrels need to be slightly fouled in order to shoot rifled slugs accurately. The traces of lead left by soft slugs on barrel walls shrink the internal diameter of the barrel to the point that subsequent slugs fit more tightly and ride more consistently to the muzzle.

The exception is rifled barrels when using sabot slugs. The slug itself never touches the barrel and the only fouling, at least with conventional velocity loads, is a slight carbon wash near the chamber. Experience with high-velocity slugs, however, has shown a perceptible plastic residue (from sabots) in the barrel that should be removed after 50-60 shots.

As noted previously, barrel ports must be kept clean in order to maintain any consistent accuracy.

So don't be discouraged about the performance (or lack thereof) of your current slug gun. The bad news is that right out of the box most slug guns won't be tack-drivers. But the good news is that most all of them can be made to shoot better.

# sighting your slug gun

Race cars can run laps in excess of 230 mph at the Indianapolis Motor Speedway, but 99 percent of American drivers couldn't get the polesitter's car past 120 mph without crashing.

The ultimate slug gun, a Remington 870 pump fitted with a Hastings barrel and a Leupold 2.5x scope mounted Scout Rifle-style on the barrel.

Today's slugs and shotguns are capable of remarkable 100-yard accuracy.

It's the same with slug shooting. Today's slugs are more accurate than most shooters. Oh, there are a few true experts who have the experience and ability to wring the absolute potential out of a gun and/or load. The rest of us rely on various degrees of approximation and luck.

Even when you're experienced it's possible to mess up. I shoot more rounds in a year than the average hunters does in a lifetime, yet the my technique is the first suspect when a gun or load isn't grouping well. Many is the time when a load wouldn't tighten inside of 3 inches at 50 yards and I was on the verge of writing it off as just another hollow claim. Then I made a minor technique adjustment and put the next several shots in one hole.

Variables? Well, one big one would be the rest. Is it solid? Can you make minute adjustments without torquing the barrel? Is the forearm rest soft enough to absorb the initial vibration at ignition?

No, a rolled up jacket on the truck hood isn't a good enough rest. You do need a steady bench and it pays to have a solid, adjustable rifle rest and rear bag.

A shotgun recoils nearly a half inch while the slug is still in the barrel and any vibration can effect accuracy. Even a loose magazine cap can throw slugs off by a matter of a couple of inches at 100 yards. Imagine the effect if you rest a pumpgun on its slide when you shoot. The receiver of a pump should rest on the bag, not the forend or slide.

Good shooting calls for more than a good position on the bench and a general knowledge of the sight picture. It takes careful practice to apply the same gradually increasing pressure to the trigger until you reach the breaking point on each shot.

Here are some suggestions for for shooting slug guns off a bench:
- Use a quality rear bag and line the recoil pad of the gun directly over the back edge of the bag.
- Keep the front sling stud 2 inches forward of the front bag.
- Pull back firmly on the pistol grip with the right hand.
- Use the left hand (just behind the rest) to pull the forearm downward and rearward at the same time.

We've all seen experts shooting rifles off benches with the gun's forearm lying on the front bag and the shooter's left hand tucked in front of him on the bench. Those guys aren't shooting 440-600-grain loads.

Tuck that left hand underneath when shooting a slug gun off a bench and you're likely to be using it next to wipe a bloody brow. A 7-pound, 12-gauge slug gun exerts approximately the same felt recoil as a .375 magnum rifle and a thin-walled shotgun barrel kicks more wildly than a sleek rifle barrel.

How about the range? Do you use wind flags? Yes, breeze is a factor even with full-ounce projectiles. A big factor. A 440-grain saboted slug will move more than half a foot from the point of aim at 100 yards with an 10 mph cross wind. Fosters wander even more.

Okay, you know the routine. You know your gun. It's a dead-calm day and you're still not satisfied with how the gun groups. Let's understand that if a commercial slug gun puts three shots in a four-inch group at 100 yards it's probably performing within the specs set by the manufacturer. MOA slugs and slug guns—not to mention shooters—are extreme rarities, regardless of what you read in magazines.

But let's also understand that 100-yard target accuracy isn't essential to the average slug hunter. Most of our shots are well inside of 80 yards at vital areas nearly twice the diameter of a basketball a difference, of an inch or two at 100 yards is moot.

When sighting in a shotgun from a bench, always grip the forearm and draw it down and back toward you.

One concession the average slug shooter should make is to shoot 50-yard ranges rather than 100. The human variable is magnified appreciably in that second 50 yards, making it much harder to make accurate judgements. If you're shooting sabots with the correct twist rate, once you get a combination shooting in the same hole at 50 yards, rest assured it will group well at 100. If you're grouping full-bore slugs well at 50, count on similar groups out to 75-80 yards.

And be happy with that.

# the ultimate slug gun

Slug guns are different things to different people.

For instance, the majority of the nation's 4.1 million slug shooters don't use a dedicated deer gun. They prefer to use one shotgun for small game, bird and big game hunting and change its purpose simply by changing loads. They typically keep their shots short, use rifled slugs and no optics.

But the folks that go to seminars, read up on slug shooting and put in their time at the range are more serious about slug shooting and tend to use guns dedicated to deer hunting. At least seasonally dedicated with aftermarket barrels, scopes, etc.

The ultimate slug gun to a deep woods stand hunter then wouldn't be the ultimate to a midwest hunter who is often confronted by 150-yard shots over CRP fields. Nor would it be the same "ultimate" to the guy who spends the day tracking and stalking big woods deer.

Accuracy is the ultimate quest for some folks while others shoot under conditions where hitting the animal isn't a problem, but they need quick cycling guns. And, again, many people want a gun for all seasons.

Oh, I'm sure that a Tar-Hunt RSG series 12- or 20-gauge slug gun would be considered the ultimate in areas—pinpoint accuracy, light to carry and short-barreled to be easily manipulated in a stand. I have Tar-Hunts and use them often—but that doesn't put me in an ivory tower, oblivious to the fact that the majority of the nation's shotgunners aren't willing or able to fork out $2,000 for a gun that can only be used for deer hunting.

Mike Jensen of Arizona took this Illinois whitetail with a Tar-Hunt custom slug gun and Lightfield Commander slugs.

My deerstand at home, for example, has produced more than 30 whitetails in the last 20 years. It's set in a second-growth hardwoods woodlot bordering the neighbor's. The shots are generally up-close-and-personal at deer moving through saplings. Although I've taken a few deer at 100-plus yards, the vast majority of the shots are inside of 60 yards.

I've used the Tar-Hunts there but I didn't need their minute-of-angle accuracy—and I also found that working the bolt wasn't as fast or efficient as a pump gun. I've got an H&R 980 bull-barreled single-shot that will shoot virtually as accurately as the Tar-Hunts, but it wasn't the ultimate because a) it weighs 11 pounds scoped; b) offers just one shot and c) is dedicated only to slug shooting.

In that stand I've used just about everything, but over the last couple of years I've settled on the "perfect" gun. It's a Remington 870 Special Purpose receiver fitted with a smoothbore Hastings barrel and a Hastings rifled choke tube. Built by a now-defunct shop in Ohio, the gun features a honed trigger and a 4x Leupold Compact scope mounted on the barrel, Scout rifle style.

My Ithaca Deerslayer II's and the Tar-Hunt DSG-12 custom 870 also served well from this stand over the years, but the extended eye relief of the barrel-mounted scope on the latest 870 gives me a much wider view of the free-fire zone.

I am also fortunate to be able to hunt big-buck, open-field states like Illinois, Ohio and Iowa, where much longer shots, higher magnification optics and more sophisticated slugs come in awfully handy. For that I install a Hastings Paradox rifled cantilever barrel and scope.

I pin the barrels in the gun to dampen harmonics and it's a great shooter. After the deer season I can, and do, hunt turkeys, varmints and even geese with the gun in its smoothbore configuration with the appropriate choke tube.

It's the Terminator; my gun for all seasons. And it would likely appeal to any slug shooter, regardless of preference.

The author's version of the Ultimate Slug Gun felled his 100th whitetail taken with a shotgun, this Illinois 8-pointer. He used Federal TruBall slugs.

# The Perfect Turkey Gun

We've looked elsewhere in this book at the ultimate slug gun. Now let's look at what the best set-up would be for shotgunning's other specialty application, turkey hunting.

My ultimate turkey gun started life as an Ithaca Model 37. The 7-pound 12-gauge featured a 25-inch fixed extra full choke barrel and a mottled paint scheme that the company at that time felt was an ideal camouflage livery, even though it looked like a third-grade finger-painting project.

Specialty choke tubes make today's guns even more effective for turkey.

I was seeking the perfect turkey gun and this was it—or at least it had potential. Twenty-some years, many changes and more than 40 gobblers later it is still a work in progress.

To be honest, right out of the box the gun threw the best turkey pattern (dense core) of any I'd ever encountered. But I'm a tinkerer. If something works well, that doesn't mean that I won't mess with it. So it was with "Long Tom."

After a discussion with Joe Morales at Rhino Chokes, I had him lengthen both of the gun's forcing cones, fit a screw-in choke system and port the barrel. Then I had the barrel cryogenically treated; installed the reworked trigger from my slug gun and added swivel studs and a sling. A coating of Realtree Xtra-Brown from Jim Crumley's Second Skin Camo gave it a whole new identity.

Later I added a fiber-optic sighting system and a recoil-reduction device in the stock. Mark Bansner has since cut me a choke tube with the right constriction to shoot Remington's Hevi-Shot; I added a Sims Vibration Labs recoil pad and am shopping about for suitable optics to bolt on the receiver for next season. Again, a work in progress.

## the "perfect" action

Your idea of the "perfect" turkey gun is likely different, since the foundation starts with your preference of action. I opted for the pump because of its simplicity and light weight. Maybe you have a thing for doubles, autoloaders, bolt-actions or single-shots—any of which can be the basis for the "perfect" gun.

*Next page:*
Linda Powell of North Carolina took her first turkey with a 12-gauge Remington 11-87.

There are more than 3 million turkey hunters today in 49 states. Alaska is the only state that has no turkeys.

Doubles are light, easy to point and carry. Over/unders aim like a rifle and their barrels are more likely to shoot to the same point of aim than a side-by-side.

Two barrels offer an instant choice between two chokes, but they are expensive and obviously limited in firepower.

If you are concerned with recoil—and turkey loads certainly do kick —your best bet is the autoloader, which uses either a mechanical system or a gas piston to suppress the kick. The autoloader is also the quickest repeating action. Autoloaders are, however, the heaviest shotguns made and are far more expensive and complicated than pumps.

How about a bolt-action? Inexpensive, simple, durable—but cycling the gun is cumbersome, which means little in turkey hunting when a single, aimed shot is the norm. Single-shots are by far the simplest, least expensive shotgun actions. They also kick harder than any other gun and follow-up shots—again, rarely needed—are problematical at best.

How about chamber size? The 3½-inch 12-gauge is the hottest thing on the waterfowl and turkey market—stuffing an extra half-ounce of shot into the .729-inch cylinder. The recoil, however, is devastating—and that extra half-ounce doesn't usually show up in a meaningful area of the pattern. The extra shot is valuable to waterfowl hunters who want a wide pattern to cover flying birds, but a turkey pattern needs to be tight with a dependably dense core—which is why the small-payload, high-velocity loads are so popular.

Suffice it to say that the perfect turkey gun doesn't need a 3½-inch chamber.

# the barrel is the soul

Elsewhere in this book we've referred to the barrel as the soul of the shotgun. It's the same with a turkey gun. If the action is the launching pad, the barrel is the directional guidance system. The quality of the barrel determines the quality of the gun.

At one time long barrels were needed to fully burn the powders of the day and provide magnum velocity and energy. Today's smokeless powders, however, burn in the first few inches of the barrel. The rest is largely ornamental and can be cumbersome when toting the gun in thick brush.

There is an increase in velocity in longer barrels but testing has shown that the advantage is very small and dies off in barrels longer than 25 inches. I prefer the longer sighting plane of the 25-inch barrel but the difference in ballistics between the longer barrels and the stubby 20-inchers is negligible in the turkey woods.

I'd also think about porting the barrel of the "perfect" turkey gun to vent gases in a specific direction, reduce barrel jump and felt recoil.

In addition, ports grab and slow the shotcup, which helps separate it from the shot column. That keeps the shotcup-wad from blowing into the pattern and tends to shorten the shot string for better pattern density.

The interior dimensions of your barrel are as important, if not more important, than the choke. Having the forcing cones extended at both ends of the barrel eases the trauma on the shot charge, giving it more room for the individual pellets to sort themselves out before traversing the tube. This also reduces felt recoil and improves patterns due to the decreased instances of deformed pellets.

Backbored or over-bored barrels are common on custom turkey and waterfowl guns but in actuality don't improve their performance. They tend to throw nice, round, even patterns but not the dense core desired in turkey patterns.

Remington SP-10 autoloading 10-gauge shotgun.

This dense 40-yard pattern would be lethal, even though it was pulled slightly to the left.

The end of a successful Texas hunt.

Today's turkey hunter has a wide and varied choice of specialty shotguns.

# the stock

The stock on the perfect turkey gun should be lightweight yet durable, which may push you in the direction of synthetic. But lightweight means that recoil will really push the gun around.

Personal preference is a heavier wood stock, maybe even a laminated model from Boyd's, that would soften recoil and give the gun a solid aiming platform.

# choke section

The perfect turkey gun would have a screw-in choke system, and the perfect choke tube would be the one that patterns your favorite load the best. Tube selection is a purely personal decision—one arrived at after serious research.

# sights

The simplicity of open sights has been a longstanding personal preference, but the tighter-patterning, longer-range loads of today require more precise aiming. Therefore I grudgingly admit that the "perfect" gun would include optics.

Few receivers are thick enough to provide sufficient purchase for mount screws, but there are saddle-style mounts that bolt to the receiver.

Virtually all optics manufacturers offer a low-or-no-magnification, illuminated dot or heads-up display suitable for turkey guns.

Action, barrel, choke, trigger, camo, optics—we've touched on virtually all aspects of the "perfect" turkey gun. All of them, that is, until a heat-seeking target-lock system is perfected.

# cosmetic surgery for your shotgun

My battle-scarred Ithaca M87 pump shotgun had a problem. Oh, it threw the best pattern with turkey and waterfowl loads of any 12-gauge shotgun I've ever encountered—an excellent hunting tool. For 10 years whenever I pointed it at a bird, the duck or turkey was as good as in the bag.

But all of that quality was cloaked in a decidedly austere livery that the Ithaca Gun Company of the late 1980s called its "Camoseal" camouflage design. It was fine for a while, and probably hid the gun well enough from the notoriously skeptical eyes of *meleagris gallopavo*, but in the early 1990s aesthetics took on a major role in the shotgun world and suddenly my effective but homely pumpgun's looks became a factor.

At that time major shotgun manufacturers started using the ColorWorks dipping process to cloak new guns with licensed camouflage designs. Suddenly, instead of hiding your gun, it was fashionable to make it more pleasing to the human eye; to match the pattern of your hunting outfit.

Personally, it didn't matter to me. The gun was a very effective, albeit ugly tool. But on a professional level, a camo job that looked like a fifth-grade art project gone sour simply didn't cut it. Since the gun was featured in magazine photos over the years I'd gone to swathing it in a variety of licensed camouflage tape designs, both to be politically correct with the magazine advertisers and to hide the now-embarrassing green-and-black ornamentation. I needed a more modern fix.

There are plenty of folks hunting with guns today that simply weren't available with a camo option, or at least not in the newest popular pattern. Luckily, there is a solution. It's called Second Skin, a process that can apply the camouflage coating of your choice by employing the same method that's performed commercially on new specialty rifles, shotguns, muzzleloaders and bows.

The price is comparable to a re-blueing and/or stock refinishing job. The pattern also protects the newly coated components from corrosion. On used guns the parts are thoroughly degreased, then painted with a base coat followed by a primer coat. When both have been dried and taped, a sheet of film is placed on the surface of an immersion tank filled with water heated to a specific temperature. The film, which holds the camouflage pattern, is then sprayed with an activator that dissolves the film, leaving the colors in the water. The gun part is dipped into the colors, which adhere to the surface.

The part is then rinsed, dried, inspected and finally sent to a touch-up room for a final finish.

Second Skin is a subsidiary of Immersion Graphics, a Georgia-based company founded by Realtree camouflage magnate Bill Jordan and a group of investors. The Japanese-designed process was discovered by then Realtree licensing chief Steve Lamboy (yeah, the guy who later founded Ithaca Classic Doubles) at an industry show in Europe and was incorporated in 1996 in Columbus, Ga. The company also puts the coating on new guns, bows, etc. for manufacturers as a competitor to ColorWorks, which until March of 1996 was the only company in that field.

Second Skin is franchised but is currently headquartered in Roanoke, Virginia, and is headed by Jim Crumley a former Trebark camouflage pioneer.

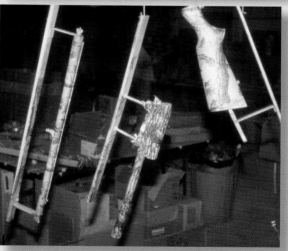

*Top:* Parts are dipped into a film bath to coat them with camouflage pattern as part of the Second Skin process.

*Below:* Gun parts drying after being coated with camouflage.

# Optics and Sights

Optics on a shotgun? C'mon, would you bother to put racing wheels on a taxicab? Honestly, the concept of shotguns under glass was virtually unheard of until relatively recently. But given the accuracy of today's slug guns and loads, and the improved chokes and barrels on other hunting shotguns, it now makes excellent sense. Today, high-tech optics are needed to achieve the guns' and loads' true accuracy potential.

In turkey woods optics are a Godsend to anyone who suffers from failing vision or perhaps a skewed barrel. Barrels or chokes that fail to shoot directly to point of aim are common among today's turkey guns, a situation that can be righted by adjusting a sighting device to compensate for defects in the shotgun.

Another element is the tight patterns thrown by today's turkey "special" loads and chokes. These make precise aiming absolutely essential. Enter specialty optics to the rescue.

Be advised that an inexpensive rifle scope isn't the solution for slug or turkey gun optics. Shotguns don't contain their concussion in the receiver like rifles do and therefore will punish a scope more than does a rifle. A cheap $39.95 "Blue Light Special" isn't likely to last long in the woods.

It takes a good quality scope to resist the punnishment dealt out by a shotgun, and the shooter is wise to select one that is designed specifically for shotguns. Most companies are making their shotgun scopes parallax-free at 50-75 yards rather than 100-150 like rifle scopes. And they are built along much more sturdy lines.

One drawback to shotgun-only scopes is that they tend to be manufactured with low magnification with small objective lenses. That means you can lose precious minutes getting on target under low light conditions. Leupold, Nikon, Kahles and a few others do, however, offer 2-7x variable shotgun scopes with a larger objective lens and Sightron has a fixed 4-power with a large objective.

A good quality rifle scope will stand up to a shotgun's punishment. Most high-end or upper mid-range rifle scopes (those costing $250 and up) are tested and are required to withstand the recoil of a .375 magnum rifle and therefore should stand up to any punishment that a shotgun can inflict. It won't be parallax-free at close range but that's a very minor

Every major scope manufacturer makes at least one version of a shotgun scope, like this Burris.

*Next page:*
Today's shotgunner has a wide selection of scopes built specially for their guns.

A Benelli Super Black Eagle with SteadyGrip topped with a Swarovski rifle scope.

Once rare, scopes on shotguns are now commonplace, even on turkey hunting rigs.

factor that most shooters wouldn't even notice.

My rule of thumb is that one should pay as much, if not more, for a scope than he or she does for the shotgun. The gun, afterall, is only as effective as the optics or sights.

Magnification for either a slug gun or turkey gun in most instances is a matter of personal preference. For most hunters 4x is more than sufficient for a hunting slug gun, but target shooters may opt for more magnification. Turkey hunters may want something with little or no magnification, with 2x the high end. Magnification may help failing eyes to identify birds and beard length but can be confusing when it comes to estimating distance and quickly establishing a sight picture.

# red dot sights

Illuminated-dot electronic sighting devices—virtually standard in combat-style pistol competitions—have also found a home with slug and turkey hunters.

Dot sights incorporate a concave lens with a thin metallic coating that reflects red light while allowing other colors to pass through freely. The "dot" reticle is simply a reflection of a light emitting diode mounted inside the sight tube. The red dot appears as if it is projected on the target. Most sights have windage and elevation adjustment with clicks at 0.5 m.o.a. Some sights have 0.25 clicks and some have 0.33 and others, 0.75 increments. Sights for firearms usually have several brightness levels.

Dot size is rated in M.O.A. (minutes of angle). One M.O.A. equals 1 inch at 100 yards, hence a 4 M.O.A. dot will cover a four-inch circle at 100 yards. It will cover 8 inches At 200 yards and 16 inches at 400 yards. Red dot sights are recommended for close to intermediate range.

The Swedish-made Aimpoint came to these shores as the first illuminated-dot sighting device in 1981. It is still the industry leader, even though virtually every other major manufacturer has its own version. Make sure your dot sight has a polarizing filter. This acts as a variable light filter adjusting the brightness of the target independent of the dot intensity. It is really valuable on a bright sunny day.

Bushnell came out with the open-tube HoloSight in the 1990s and has evolved regularly while other manufacturers have followed with versions of their own. The sight projects a heads-up image on a screen, much like the sighting system for fighter pilots. A variety of sighting patterns can be fitted to the screen and the sight won't darken in low light like traditional enclosed illuminated dot scopes.

An Aimpoint illuminated dot scope works well for deer and turkey hunters.

This Burris Speed Dot, red dot sight has adjustable brightness settings for low-light hunting situations.

When buying an electronic dot sight, check to make sure that it is parallax-free, an important consideration. That means if the scope and gun are stationary and you move your head, does the dot move on the target? If not; if the dot stays on the bull regardless of your head position, the scope is said to be parallax-free.

Also consider that under certain conditions, such as dim light (bad weather, dusk or dawn) the dot, regardless of how low you adjust the illumination, will be so bright that it will darken the screen and prevent you from aiming properly. With a snowy background or in bright light conditions, however, the illuminated dot sights are terrific.

Always use steel (not aluminum) scope rings for shotguns, since these will be able to stand up to most punishment that can happen in the field. When mounting scopes on shotguns or magnum rifles I like to add a drop of contact cement to the rings to securely lock the scope tube in place, particularly if the rings have been lapped for a good fit.

Shotguns under glass are a relatively new but necessary concept that will only improve as more and more shooters opt for optics.

# fiber optic sights

As an afterthought, other new sights for shotguns include fiber optic sights. The special plastic fiber inserts on these open sights—front and rear—absorb and channel existing ambient light to produce bright and precise aiming points. They provide the shooter greater sight contrast for quicker sight alignment, better target acquisition and a clearer sight picture.

Some shooters swear by fiber optics for wingshooting and clays, while others find them distracting and less useful. Fiber optics might be ideal, however, for dusk and dawn or other low light hunting conditions such as grouse and deer hunting where a fiber optic sight might make it easier to pickup the muzzle against a background of dark woods and brush.

Another sight available on the market is Truglo's Tritium/Fiber Optic sight containing an isotope of hydrogen that glows in the dark. The tritium illuminates the fiber optic even in total darkness and will last for years.

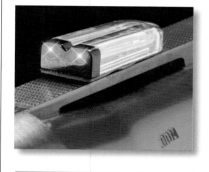

*Above right:* Examples of rear and front fiber optic shotgun sights.

*Above:* This Benelli shotgun is mounted with a red bar front sight that collects ambient light for easy visibility against dense underbrush and forest cover.

# Gun Repair and Cleaning

Whether you hunt upland birds, waterfowl, turkeys or deer or get your satisfaction at the patterning board or from busting clay birds, you will find that competently working on your own guns adds another intriguing dimension to shotgunning.

Initially, all any of us know about our shotguns is how to load it, work the safety and trip the trigger. All of the other functions are performed by a mysterious internal apparatus that has more moving parts than Janet Jackson. We just trust the invisible mechanics and probably don't give them much thought so long as the gun work properly.

For the majority of shooters that mystery remains throughout life, although probably to a lesser extent as they gain experience with the gun. But there's a small cadre of shotgunners out there who have the curiosity or need to further explore the workings of their guns.

Working on a shotgun requires the correct tools. This Brownell's tool kit is intended for Remington shotguns.

Next page:
Basic knowledge on disassembling a shotgun is very helpful for all shooters.

Sure, we've all had shotguns that misbehaved to a certain degree and wished that we could fix them. I mean, c'mon; if you've had many guns in your life, you've certainly encountered the minor inconvenience of a lost bead, bent rib, broken firing pin or split stock. You've probably had at least one with a goddawful trigger or poor sight system. Who hasn't had a ugly gun that he wished could be dressed up a little–and probably one or two handsome ones with which he couldn't hit anything?

Afterall, logic dictates that there must be a way to tame the gun that slaps the bejabbers out of you each time the trigger is tripped. Want to tighten your patterns or shift point-of-impact? Don't you get tired of the time and expense involved in taking your gun to a shop for minor repairs?

What separates the curious shotgunner from the majority of shooter/ hunters is that rather than dump the balky gun or send it off to be repaired, we had to urge or need to fix it.

The late Don Zutz, a world-class human being and one of the most knowledgeable shotgun minds I've ever encountered, once told me that if I ever got to the point where I knew enough about shotguns, then I should start over by learning to make them function correctly. Don was right; there's a parallel universe out there that pertains to shotgun repair and modifications.

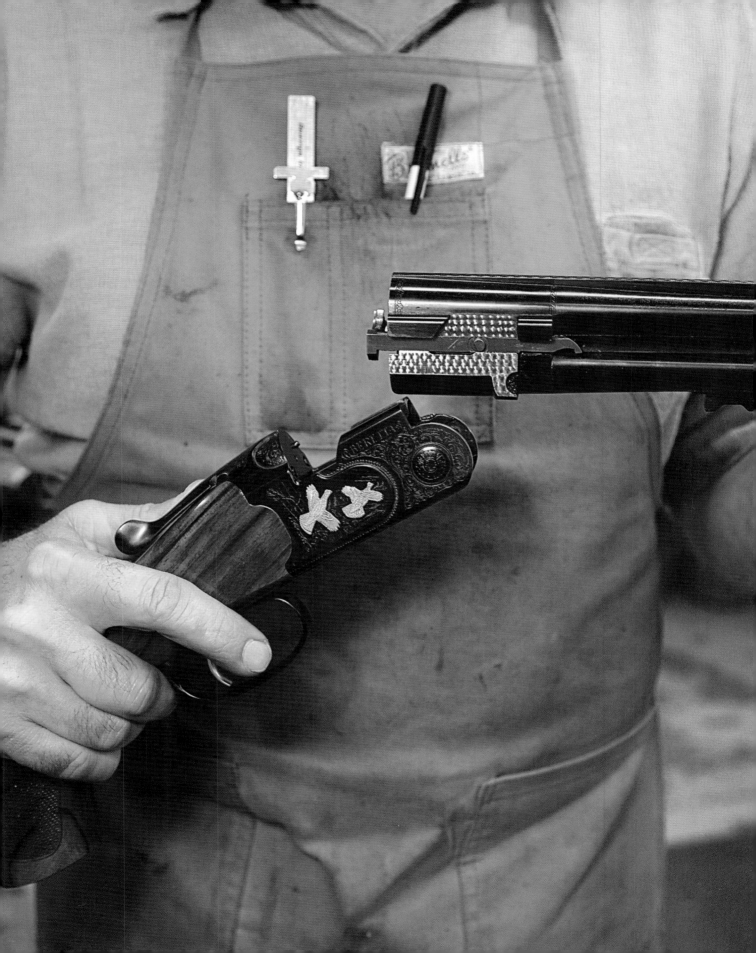

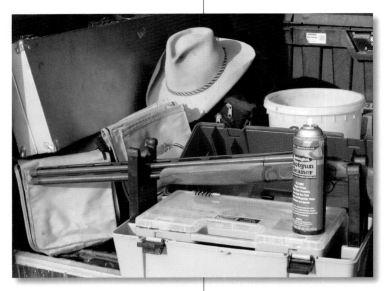

A Tipton shotgun cleaning kit with its cleaning jig is a fixture in the author's truck at shooting events and on hunts.

Researching my book, *Gunsmithing Shotguns* took me, as Zutz suggested, to that parallel world and demonstrated just how little I really knew about the hardware and assorted vagueries of scatterguns.

I am fortunate in that I have friends and acquaintances who are gunsmiths, and I was able to learn how shotguns work and found out many of their flaws just by socializing. All right, maybe it was pestering, but the knowledge derived from those sessions simply built upon my basics, which came from reading books and a gunsmithing course.

The shelves of my shop are filled with gunsmithing books and manuals but the best education I've received for working on guns came from the AGI (American Gunsmithing Institute) school. It's a comprehensive video-training course with simple, clear instruction in everything from the basics of choosing tools and setting up a shop to specific training on long guns and pistols to very specific training focused on individual models of guns.

Whenever I've had a question it was answered quickly and courteously. In many cases the instructor was able to point to a specific spot in the specific video from which I was working to illustrate his answer.

Today I've got a library of videos on specific guns that I work on most Ithaca M37, Remington 870; Remington 1100, Browning BPS and Auto-5 as well as specific tapes on my personal rifles and pistols.

I don't hesitate to work on a gun that I'm not familiar with. I just get the video on that gun and apply the skills I gained from the course.

# the basic tools

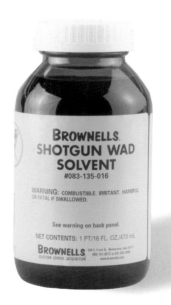

Brownell's specialty solvent works well for dissolving both powder and plastic wad fouling.

All shotguns are held together with screws and/or pins, with many "newer" American designs relying heavily on the latter.

Remington 870s, 1100s and 11-87s, for example, use a screw to hold the stock but everything else is held together with pins. The Browning Auto-5 and Ithaca Model 37, on the other hand, are two old designs that are still in heavy circulation but use screws rather than pins in the receivers.

The simple attachment systems mean that a suitable screwdriver or punch are all that's required to get the curious-but-inexperienced into trouble. But let's acknowledge that "suitable" is the operative word here. Any ole screwdriver or punch (or nail if you are of the Primitive Pete mentality) just won't do if you want to do the job correctly.

I'm sure you've read this a thousand times before but it bears repeating –when working on guns, always use the right size and type of screwdriver for the screw. Screwdriver blades should be the correct thickness and the same width as the diameter of the screw, and they should be hollow ground or parallel ground so that they fit snugly and don't slip.

Those you find at the local True Value will have tapered blades to "fit" more screws. Using them on a gun is asking for a distorted slot or marred finish, achieved when the damned blade slips out of the slot and made a free bore "engraving" run of its own.

The only instance in which a common screwdriver may be of use in a gunsmith shop is in removing the long bolt that secures the buttstock to the receiver. Most today are hexheaded bolts (7/16 is common) but a foot-long Sears screwdriver will suffice for any that still use slotted bolts.

If the screw is a Phillips head the suggestion is the same—make sure your screwdriver is the same size. Virtually all small Phillips heads will fit in all Phillips head screws but, again, using the wrong size driver is asking for problems.

A set of magazine cap pliers from Brownell's is a handy tool for anyone who wants to work on their own shotguns.

You'll see "gunsmithing" multiple-head screwdriver sets advertised in a lot of catalogs. But be advised that bits in the $20 kits are commonly too soft for heavy duty extraction work of stubborn screws.

I'm a gorilla with a screwdriver and have warped a variety of lower-priced "specialty" blades that had to be ground to another shape to regain any usefulness. Good quality gunsmithing screwdrivers are hard so that the blade will break before it deforms under load and jumps the slot.

You can throw away a lot of money, one $20 bill a time, searching for suitable screwdrivers, or you can actually save money by spending more and getting a good set.

You can't go wrong with Brownell's Magna-Tip Master screwdriver set or the Wheeler Engineering Professional-Plus set. If you're serious about working on guns, it should be a basic investment. Either will have a bit or virtually every screw you encounter and it stands up to my abuse. Fixed blade gunsmithing sets and Torx or hex head drivers will be helpful as you advance.

## punches

You'll need a set of drift punches (stronger, used with more force) or pin punches to remove and/or reset those pins.

By the way, there is nothing wrong with lubricating a pin to ease its passage into a hole, and it may pay dividends later if that pin needs to be removed. Generally speaking you should try to match the diameter of the punch with the diameter and/or shape of the pin head.

A set of punches is essential when disassembling modern shotguns.

Brass pin punches are usually recommended for drifting sights, and some guys use them on pins and other blued surfaces. Trouble is that brass pin punches can leave a residual yellow smear on a blued surface that is very difficult to remove. It's easier to avoid the situation in the first place and use steel punches.

There are, surprisingly, a lot of different types of pins in guns, and they all are used a little differently, and driven a little differently.

The simplest and most common pin is, of course, the straight pin (unhardened) or dowel (hardened). They are cylindrical and commonly

A Brownell's Magna-Tip screwdriver set will provide just about every blade needed for gun repair.

made of carbon steel.

Standard pin and drift punches are adequate for dealing with them, whether they are slave pins, slip-fit (pin is smaller diameter than the hole) or interference fit (pin is slightly larger diameter than the hole). The biggest visible difference between the two, from what I've been able to see, is that the dowel pins often have chamfered ends that allow them to be started in place easier.

Tapered pins are simply straight pins whose diameter is smaller at one end than the other. They are driven into specific holes so that they can be driven out in only one direction. They are always hardened and have domed ends and can be driven with standard pin or drift punches.

There are also, spiral, splined or grooved pins, ball-end pins, cotter, Clevis and detent pins, but you aren't likely to have to deal with them in simple shotgun disassembly.

# disassembly

## pumps

Virtually all pump guns, with the exception of the Benelli Nova can be disassembled by removing the recoil pad and loosening the long stock nut found within to detach the buttstock from the receiver. The trigger mechanism and other parts of the action are held in place with either pins or screws, or a combination of both, through the receiver.

The Ithaca M37 is one of the only pumps that still uses screws in the receiver.

With most pumps the trigger assembly drops out of the bottom of the receiver, except with the Ithaca M37, in which the trigger assembly slides out the rear when the pins and screws are disengaged.

The barrel can be removed from most models, again the Nova is the exception, by unscrewing the magazine cap, drawing back the bolt and turning the barrel until it releases. With most pumps the magazine cap is "unscrewed" counter clockwise. The Ithaca M37, however, is turned clockwise since it must be lowered to draw it out of the barrel lug, freeing the barrel. Ithaca's Deerslayer II and "Storm" models have fixed barrels that can't be removed for cleaning.

## autoloaders

The barrel can be removed from most autoloaders by locking the bolt back, putting pressure on the barrel toward the receiver and unscrewing the magazine cap.

The stock on most autoloaders—and the Browning Auto-5 is the exception here—can be disengaged by pulling the recoil pad and loosening the long stock bolt inside the buttstock. The Auto-5's stock is removed by removing a bolt that traverses the rear of the receiver.

Because of the complicated nature of the action, disassembling the action is difficult. Here again both pins and screws are used to hold the action in place and you'll find that some serve multiple functions while others are merely for structural support.

Most autoloaders can be torn down quite adequately but it takes some experience, knowledge and usually a schematic or video.

## bolt-actions

Bolt actions are universally disassembled by removing the action bolt and the trigger assembly. Barrels are threaded into the receivers.

## break-action singles, doubles

They can almost universally be disassembled by working a lever to detach the forearm, freeing the barrels to pivot downward and off the hinges of the action.

It usually takes a practiced hand to fully disassemble the inner workings of a double, but they can all be taken down to an elemental point sufficient for cleaning.

The receiver is often a sandwich of breechblock and upper tang, where the safety button is located. Unless you know the sequence of screws to remove, you may well loosen something that should actually stay tight. And putting it back together so that the safety linkage mates correctly with the button and bearing against the triggers can be frustrating if not mind-boggling.

Take it apart only if you know how or have the proper instructions. With many older guns, of course, there are no instructions and you're best advised to have someone experienced with those guns do the disassembly and assembly—and expect to pay handsomely for that expertise.

Pins and/or screws hold the action in place. All that use a stock bolt must be disassembled by first removing the bolt and stock. To find out if your double has a stock bolt, remove the recoil pad and look for the large diameter hole drilled lengthwise in the stock with a bolt head in the dark recess.

Removing the magazine cap is the first step in removing the barrel on most autoloaders, like this Browning Auto-5.

Most shotgun stocks can be removed by removing the recoil pad or buttplate and loosening the stock bolt.

# gun repair safety

Safe gun handling is a prerequisite for gun repair. Always open the action to make sure the gun is unloaded before beginning any repair work.

If you are going to work on your gun, you must know what you're doing, why you're doing it–and the safest way to approach it. This may be obvious; it may be tired–but these parameters are absolutely critical when working on a firearm.

The most elemental facet of gun repair safety is to make sure the firearm you are handling is not loaded. The second rule is, even after you've determined that it's empty, to still treat that gun as if it were loaded at all times.

That may sound trite, even condescending, but little lapses can have grave consequences when handling firearms. It's not the gun that's dangerous, it's how that gun is handled. A loaded gun lying a bench is only a harmless paper weight. But it gets dangerous very quickly when someone picks it up.

There's no such thing as being over-cautious. The NRA contends that "Guns Don't Kill People...." but they certainly can be assisted in the task.

Remember, it's always loaded. Beyond this, there are a few essential do's and don'ts involved with working on firearms.

- Always be sure that you know exactly how to perform, and feel competent in its application, before undertaking a repair. If you are not sure, seek help.
- Never eat or drink from an open cup in your shop and always clean your hands when leaving the shop. Lead and other toxic elements are likely to be in the shop air at any time and you don't want to ingest them.
- When replacing parts, make sure that the new ones function properly before attempting to fire the gun.
- Adjusting trigger pull is for experts. That's why any trigger alteration voids a gun's warranty. Don't work on a trigger unless you are well experienced with that particular model–and hone it with extreme care. A little too much can be way too much to the operator and/or can compromise the function and safety of the firearm.
- Never heat any part of a gun unless you know specifically what you're doing, and only then proceed with extreme care.
- Never take excessive amounts of metal from an action at points of stress.
- Wear safety goggles when filing, stoning, grinding, cutting, sanding or working with caustic solutions.

# let's keep it clean

A major facet of gun repair is not mechanical but rather sanitizing.

Everyone knows that firearms should be cleaned regularly. Of course we also know the virtues of low-fat foods, well-fitting shoes, flossing and safe sex, but how many of us pay attention to them?

Seriously, cleaning a shotgun after a day of hunting or shooting is like washing the dishes after a good meal–something that really ought to be done but it comes at a time when the enjoyment level has waned. Yet the performance of more guns is probably ruined by inattention to cleaning than by all other malfunctions combined.

In fact, the first step in diagnosing or fixing a malfunctioning shotgun should be a thorough cleaning–even though it may not look necessary.

Even after running a 100 trap loads through a gun, I can run a Tico brush, bore snake or a floor-mounted brush through the barrel and it will look shiny. That will fool most folks into thinking it's clean. It ain't.

You've got to realize that the foreign waste elements in your bore –plastic and newly burnished lead–are shiny too. And they are thus blending into the barrel shine, hiding there so that they can trap moisture against the steel and compromise the surface of the barrel.

Allowing the barrel to stay dirty, or not cleaning ports, also puts a drag on subsequent wads and allows the shot charge to separate before it is supposed to, resulting in blown patterns, high pressure scenarios, excessive recoil, etc.

Failing to keep the gas jets clean in an autoloader consistently leads to malfunctions.

Even if a barrel is cleaned regularly, only truly experienced shotgunners pay any attention to cleaning choke tubes, forcing cones or chambers, yet that's where pressures are greatest on the shotcup and charge and where plastic fouling builds up quickest.

Excessive fouling in those areas can be a real performance sapper. I use a Crud Buster tool to clean choke tubes and a chamber brush to scour that potential problem area. One tip: once you install the chamber brush on the handle, don't take it off. It has a larger diameter than the conventional barrel brush but looks the same and can be compressed (and thus ruined) by inadvertently using it in the bore.

Be advised that rifled barreled shotguns that fire sabot slugs will likely have fairly clean bores. The slug never touches the barrel interior and the only barrel fouling will be powder residue ahead of the chamber. If the barrel is ported, however, there will likely be a plastic build-up shaved off the passing sabots by the edges of the ports and that build-up can, and will, effect accuracy.

## selecting equipment

Riflemen are warned to stay away from hardened or stainless steel jointed rods since they can scratch a bore and mar

Cleaning and maintenance products.

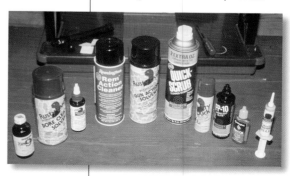

# refinishing stocks

If you rasp off a section of comb or toe or reshape a grip the alteration, you're going to have to know how to refinish the stock so that the whole thing matches.

Old finish can be removed with a chemical or electric stripper and/or sanding, after which dents and blemishes must be addressed before it can be refinished. But there is a process that both scrubs off the old finish and uses heat to fix any dents at the same time.

You'll need a bucket of hot water mixed with a half-cup of bleach and a half-cup of Mr. Clean cleaner. Wear rubber gloves and use a scrub brush to apply the solution to the stock. Rub for about five minutes, wipe the suds off with a cloth, then hold the stock over a source of heat to dry the wood.

Obviously you don't want to scorch the wood, just heat it enough to raise the grain. When you can't see any more moisture on the wood, rub the entire stock with 2/0 steel wool to clean off the "whisker" and remove more of the finish. Repeat the entire process until all signs of the old finish are gone.

The process should raise most dents in the wood. Any stubborn ones can be raised with direct application of heat as outlined elsewhere in this book. Many stocks will be ready for final sanding after three or four applications of the solution and heat. Stubborn ones, however, will take 15-20 repetitions. Concentrate on stubborn spots. If the applications don't bring all of the oil out, mix a little plain paint whiting and a grease solvent and brush it on the trouble spot. Heat the spot and when oil comes out, wipe it away and treat the area with the whiting solution.

When all of the old finish is removed, sand the stock completely, starting with medium grade and working to very fine, then polish the wood with fine (4/0) steel wool. Now clean the entire stock with an application of turpentine and allow it to dry.

There are a ton of commercial finishes available—Dem-Bart and Birchwood Casey have complete lines—including polyurethane and epoxy, but probably the best all-around finish for novices and professionals is linseed oil with fast-drying additives.

Mr. Clean and bleach are needed during stock refinishing work.

rifling. Since shotgun barrel steel is even softer than rifle steel, it makes sense to avoid the same thing.

Jointed aluminum rods are similarly unhealthy since a soft metal like aluminum can pick up grit and act just like a lap, scratching the lands and grooves of a rifled barrel or the mirror finish of a shotgun tube. I use only nylon-coated rods from Dewey or Bore Tech.

For 12-gauge shotguns a rudimentary patch rod can be made from a 5/8-inch wooden soft pine dowel with a bicycle handlebar grip fastened to one end. An absorbent paper towel (we've found Bounty brand works best) folded and rolled to bore-filling diameter is an excellent shotgun cleaning patch. Soak the towel with bore solvent and push it length of the bore from chamber to muzzle.

I shoot 12,000-15,000 rounds of trap and other loads a year, which means I'm cleaning shotguns on a regular basis. That means plenty of experience with a wide variety of bore solvents.

Very few bore solvents dissolve both the carbon residue from burnt powder and the plastic wash left behind by shotcups. Shooter's Choice MC-7 and its aerosol Xtreme Clean are absolutely the best I've encountered but Blue Wonder and Remington's Shotgun Cleaner also work.

Next, wet a bronze brush, tornado brush or even a bore brush wrapped with a copper kitchen scrubbie with bore solvent and work it throughout the bore, paying special attention to the choke and forcing cone areas.

Now run a wet patch, then dry ones until they emerge clean. If you are looking to remove plastic wad or sabot fouling use a little common sense and don't buy a solvent that comes in a plastic bottle. If it doesn't eat through a plastic container, it's not likely much threat to wad fouling.

Also, use only phosphorus bronze brushes wound on a core for shotguns. Stainless steel brushes are so hard they will score some shotgun barrel steel.

Stubborn fouling may require a vigorous scrubbing with a brush or scrubby. I've been using an Outers motorized "Power Scubber" in badly fouled bores. Prior to that I'd score a rod and wrap it with steel wool, then put the rod in a drill chuck to use as a rotary scrubber.

Badly fouled gas ports in autoloaders can be very frustrating to clean. I like to soak them in bore solvent a couple of days before tackling the job and use a gas ring or barrel hanger brush. Some gas systems have been so encrusted it took a grinding tool to dislodge the crud.

If I'm going to be storing the gun for a while, I might run a wet patch through the cleaned barrel to leave a protective film.

A functional shotgun cleaning rod can be fashioned from a 5/8 inch wooden dowel fitted with a bicycle handle grip.

## cleaning cradle

Always use a cleaning cradle to hold the firearm or barrel steady while the cleaning rod is worked. The rest should have padding to protect the finish and should be built so that the muzzle is lower than the breech so that solvents drain away from the chamber and stock wood.

MTM Caseguard makes a very good low-lying "Portable Maintenance Station" that I've used for years. It is designed to sit piggyback on a portable tool chest. Tipton also makes one designed for field use that is an actual tool chest that opens into a cradle.

I keep one of the Tipton case/cradles in the truck and it's with me at shoots or on hunting trips. A brief case-sized Remington Target Master cleaning kit is in the shop, for use with the Caseguard cradle.

## cleaning choke tubes

Screw-in choke tubes also require special attention. If they are ported, they will definitely need to be scrubbed regularly with a specialty tool like a Crud Buster and a choke tube cleaner like Shooter's Choice to get rid of wad or sabot fouling scraped off by the ports. Even non-ported tubes need extra scrubbing since they catch the full brunt of a slug being slammed into it at peak velocity, which is bound to shave and shape that slug.

Choke tubes require special attention when cleaning barrels since they tend to accumulate fouling by themselves.

I keep a stainless steel barrel tank filled with solvent year-around and soak my trap and occasionally slug gun barrels in it before giving them a thorough cleaning. Any surface rust can be rubbed off with fine steel-wool. I realize that a couple of gallons of bore solvent is a pretty dear investment but it will last for years.

A trapshooting friend makes an

affordable and suitable (yet caustic) alternative by mixing equal parts of kerosene, paint thinner, Dextron III automatic transmission fluid and Acetone.

Again, surface rust can be lifted cleanly from barrels and receivers soaked in this stuff with just a fine steel wool pad. You won't want to use this concoction in a confined shop but it works wonders in well ventilated areas.

My friend filled a parts washer with the mixture and left some parts overnight. The next day he turned on the washer motor and got no response. The concoction had dissolved the motor's plastic housing and the resultant gunk buggered the motor. See the sidebar on the mixture, known as Ed's Red Bore Cleaner.

Remember that the cleaning rods should always be wiped clean and the brushes should have solvent rinsed out of them with a degreasing agent. Solvent is meant, afterall, to dissolve gilded metal and doesn't know the difference between residue and a bronze or brass bristles.

## clean the action

So far we've only covered cleaning the barrel. You should be suitably familiar with a particular firearm that you can take it apart and clean the action, trigger mechanism and interior surfaces. It's going to require a long screwdriver or socket wrench and extension (to pull the stock), screwdrivers and drift or pin punches to disassemble the receiver and maybe a spanner wrench if you're pulling the forend off a pump. In some pumps you may want a staking tool to re-install the shell stops.

Old lubricant, carbon and primer fouling are magnets for air-borne crud and it will accumulate inside the receiver faster than outside. After disassembling the gun, use a toothbrush to scrub bearing surfaces with bore solvent to clean actions. I spray the works with an aerosol action cleaner, letting it drain off into a wad of paper towels, then wiping it off and spraying with a degreaser. You can then coat the metal surfaces with a quality moisture displacent.

Because bore solvent is so expensive, some folks use mineral spirits as a cleaning solvent to wash parts and scrub actions – however, it'll clean parts but won't clean barrel fouling. Mineral spirits as a cleaning solvent are inexpensive, non-flammable, not petroleum based and virtually odorless when new. I've gone to washing parts in Brownells d'Solve, a concentrate that can be mixed with water to create a very effective yet non-caustic cleaning solvent.

Remember that water is the Devil's personal tool when it comes to firearms destruction, but parts washed and scrubbed in a water-based solvent can be dried with a blow drier or heat gun. They should then be wiped with penetrating oil.

## lubrication overrated

In many instances, lubrication is overrated and can even become a detriment. A small amount of lubricant may help break in a new gun to ease the wear in metal-on-metal contact areas, but most folks use too much. Excess lubricant can gum up the action by attracting grime or actually impeding the action when it changes consistency in extreme conditions.

## homemade bore cleaner: ed's red

Competitive shooters have a history of concocting witches brews as alternatives to high-priced commercial products and one of the most effective homemade bore solvent/cleaning agents I've ever encountered is one adapted from an old Frankford Arsenal recipe by well-known industry figure Ed Harris, who worked with Ruger and the military.

A shooting buddy showed me a piece that Harris wrote on "Ed's Red" Bore Cleaner in the mid-1990s and I keep a bath of the stuff in a covered stainless steel barrel soaking tray in an outbuilding year-around. A word of caution: This stuff is caustic and flammable thus should only be used outside or in a well-ventilated area.

Precautions should be taken and directions should be followed exactly, but when mixed and used correctly, Ed's Red is truly effective at dissolving carbon residue, cleansing the barrel and protecting the steel finish against corrosion. And it costs a fraction of the price of commercial bore solvents.

Harris' recipe is based on proven principles and incorporates two polar and two non-polar ingredients. It is adapted from a formula in Hatcher's Notebook, Frankford Arsenal Cleaner No.18, but substituting equivalent modern materials.

The original Hatcher recipe called for equal parts of acetone, turpentine, Pratts Astral Oil and sperm oil, and optionally 200 grams of lanolin added per liter. Harris found that Pratts Astral oil turned out to be nothing more than acid free, deodorized kerosene. We substitute K-1 kerosene of the type normally sold for indoor space heaters. An inexpensive, effective substitute for sperm oil is Dexron (II, IIe or III) automatic transmission fluid.

The additives in ATFs, which include organometallic antioxidants and surfactants, make it highly suitable for our intended purpose.

Hatcher's original formula used spirits of turpentine, but cheaper and safer is aliphatic mineral spirits, a "safety solvent" used for thinning oil-based paints. It is commonly sold under the names "odorless mineral spirits," "Stoddard Solvent" or "Varsol." The lanolin is optional and Ed's Red works well without it. Here are the ingredients: One part Dexron II, IIe or III ATF, GM Spec. D-20265 or later. One part kerosene —deodorized, K1. One part Aliphatic Mineral Spirits, Fed. Spec. TT-T-2981F, CAS #64741-49-9, or substitute "Stoddard Solvent", CAS #8052-41-3, or equivalent, (aka "Varsol"). And one part Acetone, CAS #67-64-1.

Optional ingredient is one pound of lanolin, anhydrous, USP per gallon, OK to substitute Lanolin, modified, topical lubricant, from the drug store.)

### mixing instructions:

Mix outdoors, in good ventilation. Use a clean 1 gallon metal, chemical-resistant, heavy gage PET or PVC plastic container. NFPA approved plastic gasoline storage containers are also OK. Do NOT use HDPE, which is breathable because the acetone will evaporate. The acetone in ER will attack HDPE in about six months, making a heck of a mess.

Add the ATF first. Use the empty container to measure the other components, so that it is thoroughly rinsed. If you incorporate the lanolin into the mixture, melt this carefully in a double boiler, taking precautions against fire. Pour the melted lanolin it into a larger container, rinsing the lanolin container with the bore cleaner mix, and stirring until it is all dissolved.

I soak my shotgun barrels in a bath of Ed's Red for a couple of days, then work a bore brush through the barrel, scrubbing in 4-5 inch repeated strokes, to remove stubborn residue. Then I run a couple of wet patches through, then dry ones until they come out clean.

If you are using Ed's Red as a solvent on a patch, leaving it to soak for at least a minute after applying will improve its function.

You should wipe spilled Ed's Red from exterior surfaces before storing the gun. While Ed's Red is said to be harmless to blued and nickel finishes, the acetone will eat at most wood finishes.

Again, it's flammable, caustic and should only be used and stored in areas with adequate ventilation.

If a grease is rated for extreme temperatures its label will proclaim the fact. If not, beware. I use Shooter's Choice high-temperature grease which retains its viscosity in baking oven temperatures or cold too severe for humans to endure.

When using a grease or oil lubricant the rule of thumb is "if you can see it, it's too much." Use sparingly and always check the temperature range on the product label. If the range isn't listed, chances are you're holding something that turns into gunk in extreme cold weather.

It bears repeating here that any time you are faced with a misbehaving gun, a thorough cleaning will solve some malfunctions and at the very least will eliminate some potential problem areas and give you a clear track on which to troubleshoot.

# Loads for Various Uses

When it comes to shotgun pellets, size definitely makes a difference.

Get hit with a charge of double-aught buckshot at 80 yards and they may be measuring you for a pine box; but a spray of No. 8s from the same gun from the same distance across a dove field is a mild irritation.

Get hit with a single No. 6 pellet from 50 yards from a 10-gauge load or a No. 4 from the same distance fired from a .410 and the tiny gun will do more damage, despite the size of the launcher. That's because the No. 4 is larger and, at comparable velocity and range, carries more energy.

There are many uses for shotgun loads, and just as many preferences in pellet sizes.

For tactical anti-personnel purposes, buckshot, slugs, buck-and-ball loads and even military flechette loads—several tungsten slivers that fly accurately with impressive lethal range and slice through targets—are the choices. For home defense, tight short-range patterns mean more than pellet size, smaller pellets are often chosen to discourage errant shots from going through partitions and into adjoining rooms.

There are even non-lethal bean bag loads, rubber slugs and soft-tenacled ordnance for crowd dispersal and police use.

But this book will concentrate on sporting loads. In clay target shooting, for instance, Nos. 7½, 8 and 9 shot are the most popular pellet sizes. In practical shooting games slightly larger pellets are needed to knock down metal targets.

Pellets for upland bird hunting and small game are made of lead and are relatively small because it doesn't take a lot of energy or mass to snuff little critters.

Small game such as rabbits calls for field loads of Nos. 4, 5 or 6 shot. Personal preference is No. 6 for pheasants either over dogs or No. 4s when walking cover without dogs and the birds or rabbits are likely to run and flush long.

When shooting flushing quail or darting doves, or even a scampering squirrel, a much lighter load is appropriate—usually Nos. 7½, 8s or even 9s and you'll probably also be comfortable with them for grouse and woodcock in wooded environs.

Turkey loads are usually plated lead although tungsten alloys are

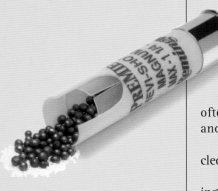

Modern shotshells utilize plastic shotcup wads that keep the pellets from touching the barrel walls and cushion the charge at setback, resulting in better performance and patterns.

Next page:
Hunters and target shooters use loads specific to their needs.

Federal's Heavyweight tungsten-alloy load patterns extremely well, thanks to the high-tech FliteControl wad.

now making giant in-roads in the market. Plated lead shot or tungsten alloy pellets for gobblers should be No. 4-5-6. There is a legion of turkey hunters using 7½ shot out there but ballistics show that those small charges in lead shot are border-line killers at distances past 22 yards and are marginally acceptable in the tungsten loads.

Tungsten-alloy shot loads like those from Remington, Hevi-Shot, Federal, Winchester and Kent carry their energy farther due to the increased density, meaning that you may be able to move to one size smaller pellet and still get increased effectiveness over lead.

The tungsten alloy loads have similarly overwhelmed the waterfowl market for the same reason. Types of loads for waterfowl are dictated by the federal government as all must be non-toxic if swallowed by feeding ducks and geese.

The size of the pellets required for hunting varies with the make-up of the pellet. We used two sizes larger in steel than in lead to get similar effect, and now serious hunters are looking at either identical-to-lead sizes for tungsten alloys or even one size smaller.

## shot sizes in inches

| Buckshot | Inches | Lead Shot | Inches | Steel Shot | Inches |
|----------|--------|-----------|--------|------------|--------|
| 000 buck | 0.360 | No.2 | 0.150 | F shot | 0.220 |
| 00 buck | 0.330 | No.4 | 0.130 | T shot | 0.200 |
| 0 buck | 0.320 | No.5 | 0.120 | BBB shot | 0.190 |
| No.1 buckshot | 0.300 | No.6 | 0.110 | BB shot | 0.180 |
| No.2 buckshot | 0.270 | No.7½ | 0.095 | No.1 | 0.160 |
| No.3 buckshot | 0.250 | No.8 | 0.090 | No.2 | 0.150 |
| No.4 buckshot | 0.240 | No.8½ | 0.085 | No.3 | 0.140 |
| | | No.9 | 0.080 | No.4 | 0.130 |
| | | No.12 | 0.050 | No.5 | 0.120 |
| | | | | No.6 | 0.110 |

Today's commercial shotgun loads range from inexpensive promotional loads to sophisticated target loads.

# loads

Load size used to be critical to patterning when shotguns all had fixed chokes. A particular gun/choke would pattern, say 1-ounce No. 6s better than 1⅛ ounce No. 6s or even or a 1¼-ounce charge of No. 4s. That scenario, however, has largely been alleviated by screw-in choke tube systems and modern shotshell components and manufacturing.

Load sizes today are largely selected by choice. In target loads a 1-ouncer may be the choice for lesser recoil, or a 1⅛-ounce load for slightly denser patterns. A turkey hunter may select a 1¾-ounce lead load for optimum velocity or a 2-, or even 2.5-ounce (in a 3⅜-inch 12-gauge) for more pellets in the count.

## greener's rule of 96

British gunbuilder William Wellington Greener was not only an innovative designer but also a respected researcher and author. His 1881 work, The Gun and Its Development is a classic that is still used as a reference book today.

The book introduced a standard that is known as Greener's Rule of Ninety-Six. Simply stated, Greener's calculations showed that a shotgun should be 96 times heavier than the weight of the shot charge it fires in order to ensure good patterns, the shooter's comfort, and the longevity of the firearm.

Applying this rule, a shotgun firing 1 ounce of shot should weigh 6 pounds. A load of 1 1/8 ounces is better suited for a 6 3/4-pound gun; 7.5-pound guns are needed to handle 1 1/4-ounce loads. Of the many pronouncements made by early gunmakers, this one is generally accepted as gospel meaning today's loads are way out of whack.

For instance, the Gospel According to Greener would dictate that the brutal but popular 3.5-inch 12 gauge of today would require a 13.5-pound gun to handle its current 2.25-ounce payload.

In a general sense, loads may also be selected by velocity—the speed that the charge is propelled down range. For reference sake, the velocity at the muzzle is used for comparison.

Muzzle velocities of less than 1,000 feet per second, for instance, are suitable for skeet (predictable targets at 22 yards) and close-flushing game while slightly higher speeds of 1,150-1,200 fps are better for trap (35 yards and farther) and wider-flushing game. Loads for bigger game, such as turkeys, waterfowl and varmints, should be 1,250-1,300 fps. Steel shot is a totally different animal and needs velocities in the 1,300-1,450 range in order to assure sufficient energy, given its lesser relative density, to kill efficiently.

Again, the velocity figures are for comparison sake only. The velocity noted on shellboxes and in catalogs are taken under ideal conditions –controlled environment tunnels at temperatures of 65-70 degrees with tight, 30-inch, 12-gauge barrels. The velocities you encounter in a windswept, icy duck blind with a 25-inch ported barrel aren't likely to approach what's printed on the box.

# how far?

A Double-Aught (No. 00) buckshot pellet will pierce human skin at 400 yards and is still lethal at 300. Ballistics charts show that the shot charge from a 12-gauge target load will drop to earth within 200 yards; larger pellets and more powerful loads will carry 300.

That's maximum range–the actual effective range of any lead shot shotgun pattern is 65 yards; 50 yards for steel; 80 for tungsten

Above: A typical shotgun wad releasing from the shot charge a few inches after leaving the muzzle.

Left: Pellet Shot Size Chart

| Shot Number | T | BBB | BB | B | 1 | 2 | 3 | 4 | 5 | 6 | 7 | 7.5 | 8 | 8.5 | 9 |
|---|---|---|---|---|---|---|---|---|---|---|---|---|---|---|---|
| Diameter in Inches | .20 | .19 | .18 | .17 | .16 | .15 | .14 | .13 | .12 | .11 | .10 | .095 | .09 | .085 | .08 |
| Pellets/oz., Lead | – | – | 50 | – | – | 87 | – | 135 | 170 | 225 | – | 350 | 410 | 500 | 585 |
| Pellets/oz., Steel | 53 | 61 | 72 | – | 103 | 125 | 153 | 191 | 243 | 316 | 420 | – | – | – | – |
| Pellets/oz., XRHD | – | – | – | 56 | – | 82 | – | 125 | 159 | 207 | – | – | – | – | – |

## high brass or low

The idea of high-brass loads being more powerful is, like many things pertaining to shotguns, a historical reference.

Higher brass on the base of the hull was a requirement when heavier doses of blackpowder or primitive smokeless powder were loaded for waterfowl, field or buckshot loads, but no longer.

Modern manufacturing techniques and materials make hulls that can withstand even the most savage loads with short brass. In fact, the height of the brass today is largely ornamental or logistical—although high brass shells may cycle and/or eject differently than low brass in some actions.

The difference between high and low brass shells today is largely a matter of manufacturing logistics, not relative strengths of powder charges as it once was.

alloys. Understand that's effective range on birds and small animals with some semblance of pattern still intact. U.S. Army specs show the effective range of Double-Aught buckshot on humans is only 40 yards.

The effectiveness of a shotgun load is measured by the cumulative energy of the pellets in the pattern. Larger gauges are deemed more powerful not because they are flying faster or farther but because they have more pellets, and thus more energy, in the pattern.

Oh, we've all heard, and a few of us have experienced, killing shots at longer distances. But those linear estimates are often exaggerated or the hits were influenced far more by luck than ballistics. The average shotgunner shouldn't attempt anything much longer than 40 yards–the average distance at which the deterioration of the pattern combined with off-center placement weakens the load's effectiveness to drop it from "lethal" to "crippling."

Wind deflects flying objects, the degree varying with wind speed and the size, shape, density and velocity of the object in flight. Shot charges are not exempt from this rule, even though wind deflection is not nearly the problem here that it is with a solid projectile at longer ranges.

Significant drift can occur, however, at 40 yards and beyond under sufficient conditions. An example provided by Winchester/Olin shows that a 10-mph crosswind will deflect 1,200 fps No. 4 lead pellets 6.56 inches off point of aim at 40 yards, 10.38 inches off at 50, 15.06 inches at 60 yards, 20.71 inches at 70 and well over two feet wide at 80 yards.

No. 4 steel, which is much lighter, is blown 8.36 inches off target under the same conditions at 40 yards, 13.21 inches off at 50 yards and 19.28 inches off point of aim at 60 yards. If you're shooting steel at 70 yards—and I'd question why—you can expect 26.80 inches of deflection and just about a yard of deflection at 80 yards.

Winchester Xtended Range and Federal Heavyweight.

## maximum practical hunting ranges

| | | | |
|---|---|---|---|
| No.2 shot | 1³⁄₈ oz | 1,260 muzzle velocity | 55 yards |
| No.4 shot | 1¼ oz | 1,330 muzzle velocity | 50 yards |
| No.6 shot | 1³⁄₈ oz | 1,165 muzzle velocity | 45 yards |
| No.7¹⁄₂ shot | 1 oz | 1,165 muzzle velocity | 40 yards |
| No.9 shot | ⁷⁄₈ oz | 1,135 muzzle velocity | 35 yards |

## what's a dram?

A puzzling part of the current shell box labeling system is the "dram equivalent" listing.

That labeling came into being years ago when shot shells were still loaded with blackpowder. For instance, a box labeled 3¼–1⅛-8 contained shells loaded with 3¼ drams of blackpowder and 1⅛ ounce of No.8 shot. Blackpowder is now obsolete yet the labeling process remains.

Today shotshells are loaded with smokeless powder and boxes are marked to show what a given charge is equivalent to in the old blackpowder dram rating. It's done for size comparison, nothing else.

But remember, smokeless powder is measured in grains and that a very small amount is equal to a much heavier charge of blackpowder. To load a shell with 3¼ drams of smokeless powder would be catastrophic.

## modern lead pellets per load

| Charge (oz) | 9 | 8 | 7½ | 6 | 5 | 4 | 2 | 1 | BB |
|---|---|---|---|---|---|---|---|---|---|
| ½ | 293 | 205 | 173 | 112 | 86 | 68 | 44 | 35 | 30 |
| ⅝ | 366 | 256 | 216 | 139 | 108 | 85 | 55 | 44 | 37 |
| ¾ | 439 | 307 | 259 | 167 | 129 | 102 | 66 | 53 | 44 |
| ⅞ | 512 | 358 | 302 | 195 | 151 | 119 | 77 | 62 | 52 |
| 1 | 585 | 409 | 345 | 223 | 172 | 136 | 88 | 71 | 60 |
| 1⅛ | 658 | 460 | 388 | 251 | 194 | 153 | 99 | 80 | 67 |
| 1¼ | 731 | 511 | 431 | 279 | 215 | 170 | 110 | 89 | 74 |
| 1⅜ | 804 | 562 | 474 | 307 | 237 | 187 | 121 | 98 | 82 |
| 1½ | 878 | 614 | 518 | 335 | 258 | 204 | 132 | 107 | 89 |
| 1⅞ | 951 | 665 | 561 | 362 | 280 | 221 | 143 | 116 | 97 |
| 1¾ | 1024 | 716 | 604 | 390 | 301 | 238 | 154 | 125 | 104 |
| 1⅞ | 1097 | 767 | 647 | 418 | 323 | 255 | 165 | 134 | 112 |
| 2 | 1170 | 818 | 690 | 446 | 344 | 272 | 176 | 143 | 119 |
| 2¼ | 1316 | 894 | 756 | 492 | 378 | 307 | 196 | 161 | 134 |

*Magnum Shot Pellet Sizes*

# hevi-shot varmint load

The shotgun is a favored tool among varmint hunters today since it kills effectively at short range, its pattern giving it an improved margin of error over a rifle, and it leaves small holes in pelts.

As with any other hunting application, the action is a matter of choice and the choke is determined by the distance of the prospective shots. Anything from slugs or buckshot (where pelt damage isn't an issue), to target loads with small furbearers. Turkey loads, particularly the tungsten-based variety, are increasingly popular because small pellets can be chosen that carry their energy and therefore lethality farther than larger lead pellets.

Author with a California coyote that wandered within 120 yards of his 20-gauge Winchester 1300 slug gun and Winchester Platinum tip sabot slug.

Occasionally an enterprising company will come up with a dedicated varmint load. Hevi-Shot's Dead Coyote load is an example, and the subject of the test in the opening scenario. It's 45 (1.25 ounces) tungsten-alloy T-shot pellets in the 2¾-inch 12-gauge load; 50 pellets (1.5 ounces) in the 3-inch version and 54 pellets (1⅝ ounces) in the 3.5-inch version. I tested only the 2¾ and 3-inch versions since the 3½s where not yet available at the time of the test.

The loads are buffered by a fine-granule grex, ostensibly to spread out pressure and cushion the pellets against each other, and trip the Oehler 43 chronograph at 1,338 feet per second on an average of 30 shots. That's surprisingly close to the 1,350 fps advertised for all three loadings. The factory claims the loads maintain 650 fps at 100 yards, with 495 needed to penetrate soft tissue.

Standard deviation is an even more impressive 7 fps; but that's a relatively meaningless figure given the fact that primers are the primary factor in standard deviation and their consistency can vary, hour-to-hour, on the manufacturing day and loading day.

As you probably know, Hevi-Shot is a proprietary tungsten-iron-tin mix that is 10 percent heavier than lead, and much harder—which promotes 20 percent better penetration in soft tissue and bone than lead. The buckshot and big-pellet loads like Dead Coyote are molded out of powdered alloy, a different process from its smaller-pellet loads, which are essentially dropped.

Hevi-Shot is produced by Environmetal of Sweet Home, Oregon. All the loading is done in white French-made Cheddite hulls with a unique roll crimp over a transparent plastic card.

## the test gun

The test gun is "The Terminator," a 12-gauge custom pump that started life as a Remington 870 but evolved into something much different with a Remington synthetic stock. The Terminator, you see, is my gun for all seasons. Honed to breaking 3.5 pounds and fitted with a wide shoe, the trigger feels and breaks like a rifle. Topped with a 2.5x Leupold long eye relief scope fitted to a rail five inches in front of the receiver on the 20-inch Hastings smoothbore barrel.

With the barrel pinned to the receiver and fitted with a 5-inch Hasting rifled choke tube, it'll shoot sabot slugs inside two inches at 100 yards. With a fully rifled cantilever barrel and sabot slugs, it'll do better than that.

With a Remington X-tra Full Hevi-Shot turkey tube installed, it's dusted at least a dozen toms, and I've even taken a half-dozen geese (all on the wing, of course) with the scoped set-up.

My test equipment includes a full array of Hastings and Remington choke tubes through which to push the Dead Coyote loads, to determine what constriction it likes best–and just what this stuff can do downrange.

## choke selection

I tried Dead Coyote's big (.020 diameter), semi-spherical T-Shot pellets through modified, full (.690 diameter), extra full (.665) and finally a special Remington Hevi-Shot Xtra full (.683) choke at 20 and 30 yards to determine which constriction was best. Fulton told me that the load would pattern most consistently through an extra-full choke, but I was skeptical. Pushing big pellets through a tight constriction is usually a problematical situation.

But surprisingly the big pellets patterned most consistently out of a super-tight Remington Xtra full Hevi-Shot turkey choke tube–only slightly more consistent than the even tighter .665 tube. All of the patterning findings were double-checked and confirmed with an Ithaca M37 with a 24-inch barrel featuring lengthened forcing cones.

Shooting 20 patterns at each yardage, I found that at 30 yards a 24-inch-square piece of paper could catch all of the load's pellets and the total dropped to about 85 percent at 40 yards and averaged about 64 percent at 50 yards. An average of less than half the pellets hit the paper at 60 yards.

The core of the patterns, however, were a different story. Using 10-inch diameter Shoot-N-C targets to approximate the vitals of a coyote on each target sheet, the gun and loads averaged 18 pellets in the black at 30 yards, about half that at 40 yards and between 6 and 7 pellets in the vitals at 50 yards.

We all know that the measure of a load's effectiveness is the cumulative energy of pellets it puts on target. Of the 20 patterns shot at 70 yards, one actually put five pellets in the vitals–but four of those patterns also had nothing in the black. In fact, it often took three shots to get even two pellets in the vital zone and the 20-shot average was two pellets in the kill zone and 14 in the 22-inch square.

The target mediums were selected based on my experience. The 20-gauge sheet metal basically just tested the hardness and brittleness of the pellets while I found that if pellets passed through the quarter-inch plywood they'd also pass completely through a coyote, making a second set of holes, which is not a desirable trait for fur takers. But passing through the eighth-inch paneling only assured that they'd penetrate the chest and organs of the dog without blowing out the far side.

The big, hard pellets blew through the boards at 40 yards. The plywood stopped the pellets at 50 yards but they still went through the paneling there, as well as at 60 and, yes, Hevi-Shot's claims were substantiated when the pellets penetrated the paneling at 70 yards. Only two pellets hit within the 10-inch outline on that particular shot, but they did penetrate.

The results of the test screamed to me, "this is impressive stuff. It's definitely not a 70-yard load; in fact, it's borderline at 50 yards, but is very effective within the parameters of common sense."

A 50-yard pattern for Hevi-Shot Dead Coyote. *Inset:* Hevi-Shot's Dead Coyote load features a rolled crimp and transparent plastic card.

A 30-yard pattern for Hevi-Shot Dead Coyote load. *Inset:* Hevi-Shot 2¾- and 3-inch 12-gauge loadings.

# What About Buckshot?

Buckshot is an up-close-and-personal load essentially for big-game hunting.

It has been a popular and effective load since blackpowder days and is still the load mandated for deer hunting in specific areas of at least 10 states. It's legal in 29 states, although five of them don't have any whitetails.

It's also a dandy anti-personnel load. So effective, in fact, that the Germans pushed to have it outlawed for warfare (yes, there are international laws for such things) at the Hague Convention after seeing its devastating effects in World War I's trench warfare.

Like all shotgun loads, buckshot has improved markedly in the last couple of decades. Development of the shot cup, copper plating, improved lead-antimony mixes and granulated plastic buffering have turned the once willy-nilly patterning characteristics of buckshot into an even more devastating tool.

Previously, users of No. 00 (double-aught) buckshot found patterns extremely ragged at close range–to the point where a deer-sized target might be missed altogether at 40 yards.

Like any shotgun scatter load, the problem is that the bigger the pellet (00 pellets are .33 caliber) the less room it has to negotiate in the crowded confines of a shotgun bore. Backbored barrels will give demonstrably better patterning than conventional diameter barrels with smaller pellets. In the old days the majority of the soft, unplated pellets were damaged or worn by the barrel walls as they sorted themselves out en route to the muzzle.

A load of copper-plated buckshot releases from the wad and heads down range. Effective patterning of lead buckshot breaks down after 40 yards.

Because of this, many buckshot hunters, in those days, opted for smaller shot such as No. 4 (.24 caliber), which patterned much denser than the larger shot. The lethality of No. 4 shot, however, is questionable beyond 20-30 yards.

If you talked to old-time buckshot hunters, full choke was the only logical choice. But with today's improved choke systems, and with the plastic sleeves and buffer keeping the shot from being deformed in the barrel, good patterns can be obtained with modified or even improved cylinder choking.

New loads, including the relatively new No. 000 (.36 caliber pellets), are more effective than ever in open-choke guns, too, for the same reason.

With today's loads, effective patterning ranges have lengthened appre-

*Next page:*
Modern buckshot loads contain grex to buffer the copper-plated pellets against each other and even out pressures.

Conventional buckshot's effective range is about 40 yards with tungsten-alloy buckshot about 60, provided the patterns hold together at those ranges.

ciably. For instance, No. 00 today, fired through a full-choke 12-gauge barrel, would probably average 50 percent (six of 12 pellets) in the traditional patterning target of a 30-inch circle at 70 yards. Just 10 years ago a 50 percent pattern could be achieved at no longer than 40 yards.

But please note that I'm talking about "effective patterning ranges," This is not an endorsement of or suggestion that one take 70-yard shots with buckshot.

Back to patterning. While a 30-inch pattern is a fine criteria for wing-shooting birds, we're aiming at 12- to 16-inch vital area in a deer. A pie plate is a better target.

Test a variety of loads and you'll find that a tiny change in choke constriction or shooting distance can make a major change in the load's pattern.

Consider that differences in the length of forcing cones in various guns, plus the differences in barrel and choke diameters, or whether a gun is backbored is going to make a dramatic difference in how a particular load performs.

I've hunted deer in areas that mandated the use of shotguns all my life, a few times where buckshot was de rigeur. Yes, I've been successful with buckshot and have no horror stories to relate about wounded animals or missed opportunities. But one day of range-testing convinced me that my success was as much a case of good fortune as it was prime (read: short-ranged) opportunity.

Sure, buckshot loads today are better than ever but as far as I'm concerned anything beyond 35 yards is a definite "maybe." Remington's introduction of Hevi-Shot buckshot may eventually change all this, but right now buckshot is most effective within basic archery ranges. And with some load-choke combinations, 20 yards might be too far.

Every time I do a shotgun seminar I hear a few stories of buckshot bringing down bucks with 60- or 80-yard shots. Yes, it can be done. But I'd never suggest it and ethical hunters shouldn't condone it.

Given the rapidity with which a single, semi-round pellet slows and thus sheds it energy, I have to say that the aforementioned 35-yard envelope is based more on ballistic surety than a luckily-placed pellet.

If you have to shoot buckshot, absolutely, positively do your homework. No relative, neighbor, magazine writer or store clerk can accurately tell you what load(s) your gun and choke will handle best. You'll probably be surprised how badly some sizes perform and how well others do. Try a variety of shot sizes (No. 00 is probably the most versatile and effective) and a variety of chokes (extended chokes seem to outperform conventional screw-ins) before making a decision. And remember when patterning that a 10-inch pie plate is a far better judge of buckshot effectiveness than the traditional 30-inch circle.

Also remember that regardless of pattern density, a buckshot pellet has the ballistic coefficient of a bowling ball. It loses energy and effectiveness very quickly and with most loads, beyond 40 yards you're hopes of success are based on a very lucky strike from a stray pellet–definitely not a trait of an ethical hunter.

Buckshot comes in seven sizes from No. 000 (8-10 pellets, .36 caliber in 12-gauge hull), No. OO (9-18 pellets, .33 caliber), No. 0 (9-12 pellets, .32 caliber in 12-gauge hull), No. 1 (16-24 pellets, .30 caliber in 12-gauge hull), No. 2 (16 pellets, .27 caliber), No. 3 (21 pellets, .25 caliber) and No. 4 (27-54 pellets, .24 caliber). The number of pellets may vary with manufacturer and length of the hull. American shotshell manufacturers usually reserve No. 2 and No. 3 shot for 20-gauge loads.

Yes, buckshot is and always has been an effective load for deer hunting. But only in the hands of those who know and abide by the load's limited effectiveness.

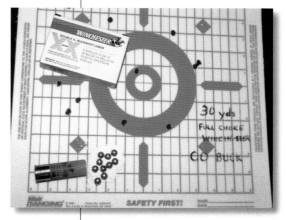

Buckshot patterns deteriorate rapidly with distance, and should be monitored closely to determine maximum effective range.

Remington makes several buckshot loads.

## buckshot sizes

| | |
|---|---|
| 000 buck | 0.360 inches |
| 00 buck | 0.330 inches |
| 0 buck | 0.320 inches |
| No.1 buckshot | 0.300 inches |
| No.2 buckshot | 0.270 inches |
| No.3 buckshot | 0.250 inches |
| No.4 buckshot | 0.240 inches |

| Shot Number | 000 | 00 | 0 | 1 | 3 | 4 |
|---|---|---|---|---|---|---|
| Diameter in Inches | .36 | .33 | .32 | .30 | .25 | .24 |
| # Pellets Typical Loads | 8,10 | 9,12,15,18 | 12 | 12,18,20,24 | 20,24 | 27,34,41 |

Buckshot Size Chart shows shot number, diameter and number of pellet in typical loads.

# Slug Shooting Today

"State-of-the-art" is a rather nebulous phrase as it pertains to slug shooting, with vastly dissimilar definitions.

For example, I took a pretty good 8-point Iowa buck in 2004 at 130 yards using Remington's 3-inch, 12-gauge BuckHammer slug and a Remington 870 TH-Slug rifled barrel pump gun with a Boyd's thumbhole stock, topped with a Nikon Monarch 3-9x40mm scope. Certainly a "state of the art" slug-shooting set-up.

A month earlier, hunting in Pike County, Illinois, where shotguns are similarly mandated, I drew down on a big 9-point buck, using another "state-of-the-art" rig–a smoothbore 870 with a 2.5x Leupold pistol scope mounted Scout Rifle-style on the barrel. That was 91 yards and the load was Federal's new TruBall load for smoothbores.

A month prior to that it was South Carolina, where, although rifles were legal, I opted for one of Remington's new synthetic-stocked 11-87 Sportsman autoloaders, topped with a 2.5-10x Bushnell 4200 scope and loaded with a Managed Recoil version of the Remington BuckHammer slug. The distance there was a testy 146 yards.

All three scenarios resulted in clean, one-shot kills. All three slugs must be considered "state of the art."

The two Remington BuckHammer slugs represent opposite ends of the spectrum in today's designs. The 3-incher is a 1,500 feet per second, 1 1/8-ounce thunderclap that generates 3,232 foot pounds of energy at the muzzle, while the Managed Recoil version is 1,350 fps and a much gentler but still effective 1,991 foot pounds of energy.

The Federal TruBall is essentially the first major step forward in slug shooting for smoothbores since the rifled slug was introduced in the 1930s and effectively increases the effective range of the industry's most popular slug design. More than 65 percent of the market is still smoothbore shotguns and rifled slugs.

The BuckHammer line similarly expanded with 3-inch 12-gauge (1 3/8 ounce compared to 1 1/8 in the 2 3/4-inch BuckHammer) and 3-inch 20-gauge (one ounce slug) versions of the big slug. Federal's new Tru-Ball slug also comes in a Reduced Recoil (1,300 fps) 12-gauge version, as well as a 20-gauge version.

Hastings offered 12- and 20-gauge slugs based on the Sabot

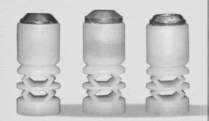

The Rottweill Laser Plus, Hevi-Shot and Lightfield Commander sabot slugs are similar in design in that their sabots remain with the projectile all the way to the target rather than dropping off en route.

*Next page:*
The author took this Arkansas buck with a Winchester Platinum Tip slug and a Browning Gold Hunter shotgun.

Technologies Hammerhead sabot design, then added a unique 3½-inch, long-range 20-gauge design and special Long Range Hunter shotgun before it went out of business in 2009. Rottweill picked up the sabot design (but not the 3½-inch 20- or the gun) for its Laser Plus design in 2011.

Hornady introduced the first polymer-tipped slugs, the SST, in 2004 and Winchester (XP3), Federal (Tipped Barnes Expander) and Remington (Accu-Tip) followed with their tipped versions shortly thereafter.

The Iowa cornfield buck was flattened by nearly 1,500 foot pounds of thunder. The 1.25-ounce, 3-inch Remington BuckHammer slug, which carries more energy than any other lead slug on the market, drove though his chest, high through both lungs and the off-side shoulder, coming to rest under the skin mushroomed but still 100% intact.

The big BuckHammer offers rifle-like ballistics of nearly three-quarters of a ton of retained energy and, fired out of Remington's 20-inch, thick-walled rifled barrel, uncanny accuracy at 100 yards and beyond.

# the truball

The TruBall is not a 100-yard-plus load like the sabots on the market. Afterall, it's still a rifled slug. But the unique design improves accuracy to the point where it will be on target at considerably longer range than its short, stubby brethren.

The polymer ball inserted in the rear of the TruBall slugs keep it from collapsing and forces it down the bore concentric with the tube, giving it a far better chance of flying true when it exits the muzzle. Because it's flying true, it remains stable farther down range.

Its Low Recoil version joins the Managed Recoil BuckHammer and Slugger designs and Lightfield Lites in the kinder-gentler genre that still provides accuracy and sufficient lethal energy out to nearly 100 yards – or much more as the South Carolina buck showed.

The Iowa buck in the opening scenario was the 102nd deer I'd taken with a shotgun. Comparing slugs and shotguns from my early days of hunting more than three decades ago with today's state-of-the-art, controlled expansion projectiles is like juxtaposing the Wright brothers' Kitty Hawk flying machine and the Space Shuttle.

In my salad days we transformed rabbit guns in to deer guns by simply changing the fodder. You bought slugs from a hardware store bin at a dime apiece with no regard to brand or type. Today we're actually comparing ballistic coefficients in shotgun loads,

*Inset:* The Federal TruBall system includes a polymer ball inserted into the rear of a rifled slug.

*Below:* A Federal TruBall slug flies through plywood (right), while the pusher wad rebounds.

for God's sake, and slipping the safety off when a buck appears two football fields away.

The aforementioned Remington BuckHammer, Brenneke's Black Magic, Gold and K.O. Sabot are all fairly new, big, full-bore, soft lead slugs that launch at 1,500 to 1,700 fps. They are made to penetrate and impart major shock on the animal while retaining most, if not all, of their mass.

At the same time, Hornady's SST, Federal's Tipped Barnes Expander, Winchester's Partition Gold and Dual Bond, Remington's Accu-Tip and CoreLokt Ultra and the Winchester Platinum Tip are all high-velocity, jacketed, lead core bullets encased in cup-like sabots.

The 3-inch Lightfield Commander and Lightfield Hybred Elite, Hevi-Shot Sabot, the Federal Barnes Expander, Remington Copper Solid and Brenneke Super Sabot are also certainly state of the art without fitting neatly into either sabot niche.

The TruBall system, Rottweil's Equal and Winchester's Super-X Power Point rifled slug are designed for smoothbore shotguns. They'll shoot fairly accurately through rifled bores, but the soft lead will skid on the rifling and quickly (within 3-4 shots) fill the grooves, after which accuracy will be compromised.

Don't shoot sabot slugs through a smoothbore gun. Sabots are designed to be spun by rifled barrels. Shoot them out of a smoothbore and the sabot sleeves aren't likely to release efficiently, which means very poor flight characteristics and greatly reduced range.

The TruBall slug separates from pusher wad down range.

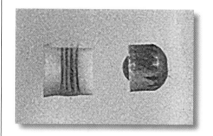

The unique Federal TruBall slug carries its ball plug down range after separating from the pusher wad. *(credit Federal Cartridge)*

# rifled barrels

If you shoot a rifled barreled slug gun, the evolution process for your slugs has been much shorter and more rapid. In the 1990s, when rifled bores were legalized in more and more states, the development of the sabot slug took a quantum leap forward.

Sabot slugs are smaller diameter (usually around .50 caliber for 12-gauge and .45 caliber for 20s, although designs use larger diameters and thinner sabot sleeves), more aerodynamic slugs encased in bore-filling fall-

Conventional velocity slugs for rifled barrels: (Left to right) Hastings Magnum, Hevi-Shot Sabot, 1-ounce Federal Barnes Xpander, Remington BuckHammer, Remington Copper Solid, Brenneke Super Sabot, Federal Premium Sabot, Winchester Hi-Impact Sabot, Brenneke Magnum.

High velocity slugs for rifled barrels: (left to right) Federal Barnes Xpander–3/4 ounce, Remington CoreLokt Ultra, Hornady SST, Hornady H2K, Winchester Platinum Tip, Winchester Partition Gold, Lightfield Commander.

away plastic sleeves called sabots. This allowed the ballistically cavernous shotgun bore to throw a much more efficient projectile–and the plastic sleeves grabbed the rifling and imparted a stabilizing spin on the whole unit.

The sabot's true advantage comes farther down range where the combination of spin and weight distribution keep it stable–thereby retaining its energy well past the point where the full-bore slugs had petered out–past 100 yards.

There have been dozens of sabot designs introduced over the last 20 years, only to ultimately fade into obsolescence. The high retail price and rapidly advancing technology combined with technical difficulty in coordinating the separation of the slug and sabot, manufacturing problems and sometimes less-than-spectacular performance doomed many versions.

The flashiest of the new sabot designs are the high-velocity (1,800-2,000 fps) versions that incorporate a big-bore, usually jacketed, lead core pistol bullet. The fastest was Hornady's H2K Heavy Mag, which topped 2,000 fps regularly but never showed good accuracy. It was retired in 2005 in favor of the new SST slug–which is the first shotgun load to use a pointed bullet design.

The SST, which has a proven accuracy record as a muzzleloader bullet, is an inch-long, 300-grain, .50-caliber version of the company's famed polymer-tipped pistol bullet that is launched at 2,000 fps.

In 2004 Winchester introduced the 3-inch 12-gauge version of its Partition Gold sabot slug with a muzzle velocity of 2,000 fps. Remington's one-ounce CoreLokt Ultra and Federal's 3/4-ounce Barnes EXpander are legitimate 1,900 fps loads and Winchester's 400-grain, 1,700 fps Platinum Tip slug is actually a .50-caliber variant of the company's Fail Safe bullet line and is virtually identical, albeit larger caliber, to the company's pistol bullet line.

The Federal TruBall is the first significant breakthrough in rifled slug performance in more than 70 years.

All offer flat trajectory, plenty of retained energy out past 150 yards and excellent upset performance on deer. The drawback is that they are not accurate in all guns. Some experts contend that a faster rifling twist (typically 1-turn-in-28 inches as opposed to the conventional 1-in-35) is essential in handling the high-velocity slugs. In fact, American Barrel Company's new fast-twist (1-in-25) shoots Federal's 3/4-ounce Barnes Xpanders with astounding accuracy.

But others will tell you that, given the pressures generated by the higher velocities and the hardness of the bullet-slug at setback, sabot-to-barrel fit (rather than twist rate) is more critical with the faster slugs than it is with the softer, slower sabots.

In fact, the difficult-to-control nature of the high-velocity slugs is probably the reason that the industry has put more design work into the more predictable full-bore sabot slugs in recent years.

The Rottweil Laser Plus (using the Sabot Technologies Hammerhead slug identical to the now-discontinued Hastings Laser) is a 1¼-ounce, 1,500 fps soft lead slug encased in a non-discarding sabot and attached wad, the sabot sleeve working like a jacket on a rifle bullet. The soft lead and flexible sabot allow it to swell at setback and thus fill the bore of any gun in which it's chambered, giving it a reputation for accuracy.

The less-accurate Hevi-Shot slug actually uses the same sabot, hull and primer as the Rottweil Laser Plus, but its slug is a much harder tungsten-alloy instead of lead. The Rotweil and the 3- and 3½-inch Lightfield Commander's sabot is of a similar non-discarding design with a different lead slug and higher (1,800-1,900 fps) velocity.

Brenneke's Black Magic and Gold slugs are, like the Remington BuckHammer, full-bore slugs with attached plastic wads but no sabot sleeves. The 1³/₈-ounce Brenneke versions are specially coated to reduce leading in the bore and offer 1,500-1,600 fps muzzle velocities in the 2³/₄- and 3-inch designs. The Brenneke K.O. Sabot is a one-ounce slug with an encompassing sabot, different attached wad and faster velocities.

Back in 1997, when Federal first started loading a proprietary soft copper version of the Barnes XBullet as the Federal Barnes EXpander, it marked the first actual bullet (rear-weighted) loaded as a slug that expanded readily. Four years earlier, Remington's original Copper Solid was the first rear-weighted, bullet-like slug design but it fell out of favor because problems caused by its uncompromising hardness.

A pile of rifled slugs as they come off the swaging machine.

## correct handling of slugs is key to performance

Temperature and moisture have profound effects on slug performance. I've seen slugs stored in a drafty shed over the winter lose more than 300 feet per second when fired the next spring. Not only do atmospheric conditions effect powder but plastic hulls (roll crimps) and sabots (dimensions) also change with temperature and humidity.

The garage, wood shed, barn, etc. is definitely not the place to store slugs. Even if they've been stored correctly in a sealed container, if you open it and leave them in the trunk of your car for a few days, the ballistic characteristics are bound to change.

But if you have a batch of slugs that gets fouled, don't throw them out or give them to your no-account brother-in-law. Storing them in a climate-controlled setting—in a room with a dehumidifier—for a few days will likely dry them out enough to perform well again. Keeping them in the house during the winter, where the temperature is relatively constant and the humidity is low, is the ideal. But what do you do when the humidity of spring and summer hit?

Try packing them in air-tight covers—Zip-Loc bags are fine

—and storing them in a cooler with a tight lid. I keep all my trap-loads in a cooler and they shoot to the same velocity whether it's in a mid-summer registered shoot when it's 90 degrees or in winter league competition when it's apt to be 80 degrees cooler.

Granted, if you're only shooting slugs 40-50 yards at a buck, the difference in performance isn't likely to be noticeable. But there will be a difference, nevertheless.

If your slugs lose or gain 300 feet per second in velocity, it translates to thousands of pounds in chamber pressure. A shift of 2,000-3,000 pounds in a rifle, where chamber pressure is 50,000-60,000 foot pounds, is inconsequential. But a shift that size in a shotgun chamber, where pressure is usually less than 12,000 foot pounds, and the percentage of loss is significant—and can translate to several inches difference in elevation 100 yards downrange.

Slugs are loaded under controlled conditions of extremely low humidity and high temperature—making them "hot" ballistically. The reasoning is that the slugs will take on moisture during shipping and storage and velocity will fall into the specified range.

Remington redesigned the Copper Solid as a virtual ballistic twin of the Federal Barnes EXpander in 1998, but when Federal sped up the Barnes EXpander as a high-velocity version in 2000, Remington took its technology toward the CoreLokt Ultra—a .50-caliber verison of its vaunted rifle bullet design.

The unique design of the Brenneke Super Sabot doesn't allow it to fit into any particular niche. A sliding copper sleeve around a soft-nosed needle core gives the 1,526 fps slug (in the 3-inch version) excellent stability, structural integrity and good expansion on impact.

# the smoothbore

All that being said, the smoothbore slug still represents more than 65 percent of the slug-shooting market. The TruBall, based on an idea patented by Georgia slug innovator Jay Menefee, is a simple yet ingenious expansion of a 70-year-old design.

Full-bore slugs for smoothbores: (left to right) Rifled slug, Original Brenneke, Brenneke Gold and Activ.

Understand that the typical rifled slug has not changed, in a visual sense, since ballistician Karl Foster's design was picked up by Winchester-Western and hit the market in the 1930s. It's still a cup-shaped dollop of soft lead with "rifling" groves swaged into the outside walls.

The TruBall's unique design—essentially a polymer ball inserted into the cavity of a conventional rifled slug and driven at 1,600 feet per second by a cylindrical polymer pusher wad—doesn't make the new slug any more powerful than conventional rifled slugs. But it does make the slug much more effective. In a comparative sense, the TruBall is not a reinvention of the wheel, but rather a move that essentially makes the wheel rounder; more efficient and effective.

The Tru-Ball extends the rifled slug's effective range since the design essentially guarantees concentricity to the bore and thus an undeformed emergence and subsequently truer flight.

Not to be left behind, Winchester introduced the Super-X Power-Point, a more stable version of the conventional one-ounce rifled slug. The Power-Point is launched at a muzzle velocity of 1,700 fps. Unlike other rifled slugs, the Power-Point's "rifling grooves" extend up the sides of the slug to the start of the deep hollow point nose.

Winchester's newest move into the rifled slug design came one year

Slugs for smoothbore shotguns: (left to right) Rottweil Blitz, Brenneke K.O., Brenneke Black Magic, Brenneke Gold, Original Brenneke, Winchester Super-X Power Point, Federal TruBall, conventional rifled slug.

after Remington introduced a high-velocity (1,800 fps in 2¾-inch and 1,875 in 3-inch) version of its venerable Slugger rifled slug line. The Slugger HV is actually a reintroduction of the company's ⅞-ounce slug that was retired in the 1980s in favor of 1-ounce versions.

Remington, Winchester, Federal and Hevi-Shot all offer various versions of the conventional rifled slug design while Brenneke, Dynamit-Nobel, PMC, Fiocchi, Challenger, Wolf and others offer full-bore designs with attached wads that are designed to be shot through smoothbore barrels.

As with all slug loads, the only way to determine the best performer in your gun is to shoot several. Today's slug shooter shouldn't have any trouble finding one that fits his needs.

# bullet-like slugs

For a long time manufacturers resisted making any slug that even looked like a bullet out of fear of rejection by lawmakers who mandated shotguns over rifles. Remington's first Copper Solid was a departure in that it was a rear-weighted bullet-like design machined out of solid copper bar stock.

When the design was accepted without objection, controlled expansion bullet designs—first the all-copper Barnes Xpander, then the jacketed Winchester Partition Gold, Hornady Heavy Mag, Winchester Platinum Tip and Remington CoreLokt Ultra. But all were relatively blunt, hollow-point bullets.

The SST's polymer tip not only serves to accentuate expansion, like a hollow point, but also gives the slug a much sleeker profile and thus excellent ballistic coefficient. It's the first-ever pointed bullet loaded in a shotgun slug, its one-inch (actually about ¹⁵/₁₆) length allowing it to be

The 2,000 fps Hornady SST is the first slug to use a polymer tip and pointed nose.

seated deep enough so that the polymer point is recessed inside the hull, far from the primer of the slug ahead of it in the magazine.

When Winchester (Partition Gold) and Remington (CoreLokt Ultra) vaulted into the 1,900-2,000 fps stratosphere they had to reinforce the floor of the sabot by molding in metal wafers to withstand the higher pressure. Otherwise the sabots would cling to the slug and not release consistently.

Instead of molding a piece into the sabot floor, Hornady places a loose cushioning wad under the slug's base to achieve the same effect.

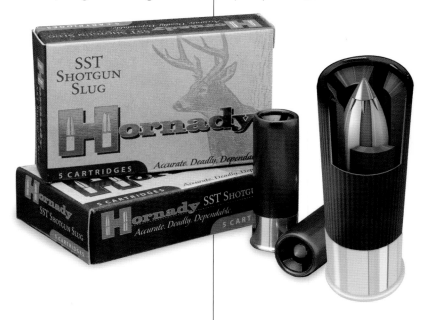

# Why Reload Shotshells?

Just taking a box of shotshells off a dealer's shelf keeps pellet sizes, powder charges and their applications abstract. Studying the various sizes and parts of a shotshell and considering the conditions under which they will be used connects the shooter with all of the elements of the sport.

By personally handling and assembling all of the components that collectively make up a given load, a shooter is more in touch with the requirements of the shooting conditions.

He plans, handles and assembles each load and reaps the subsequent sense of pride and accomplishment when that load performs well. It's probably the same reason a woman knits a sweater or crafts a quilt when good quality commercial variations are available; the same reason people build their own cabins or boats rather than contracting to have it done. It's the same reason, come to think of it, that I hunt rather than accept my meat butchered and served up between Styrofoam and Cellophane.

And hell, reloading saves a ton of money, right? Well, not necessarily. In fact, it's only economical under certain circumstances. You can, afterall, buy useable loads at WalMart cheaper than you can load 'em. The inexpensive foreign-made or American "promotional" loads with high standard deviations and cheap dropped shot are fine for most small game hunting, skeet or short-range sporting clays applications. That's what they are for.

Where you can save money is reloading sophisticated and expensive target loads—the Remington STS, Winchester AA or Federal Gold Medals. Check their ballistics in your load book and look at the tables to duplicate them, using the same hulls, wads, primers and high-antimony magnum shot, and you'll probably save 20-30 percent off retail.

That's the reason you see the mob scene at 7 a.m. when they are selling spent hulls at the Grand American trapshooting championships each August. Premium once-fired hulls at about $5 per 500 is a big draw for those who reload thousands of rounds a year.

I shoot 12,000-15,000 trap loads a year, which would be an absolute impossibility at retail. Even joining in with other shooters and buying wholesale shells by the pallet would be too expensive. Granted, mine is a special case because of indulgent contacts in the industry, but buying primers and shot wholesale and playing contacts for "bargains" in wads and powder, I can save 60-70 percent off the near-$6/box retail.

A 28-gauge slug for handloading (above left) and an 8-gauge slug for kiln guns.

*Next page:*
A handloader's grab-bag of shotshell hulls. Some are worthy of reloading while others are destined for the recycling bin.

# another reason

Even if they aren't saving much, a lot of folks reload because it gives them the ability to tailor a load to their wants and needs. Customizing ammunition to reduce velocity levels for lower recoil or adjust shot size and charge weights for specific purpose and performance are advantages afforded the reloader.

There's always someone looking for something different. You can't, for instance, find 28-gauge slugs or 10-gauge sabots, or hard-hitting .410 loads—but they can be handloaded.

Catalog houses like Ballistic Products Industries (BPI) and Precision Reloading offer specialty components, instructions, books, load data and equipment to make loading everything from cheap practice loads to the most obscure specialty loads achievable.

Elsewhere in this book you'll read about my 80-plus year-old, 6½-pound Ithaca 16-gauge side-by-side. It's a carrying gun, meant to travel easily and swing with grace; a light field piece that wasn't designed to handle magnum loads. Hell, the chamber had to be lengthened before it would even accept modern ammunition. Try finding a good-quality light commercial load for a 16-gauge gun today.

Since the gun doesn't get fired more than a couple hundred times a year, loading speed isn't a factor. A MEC Sizemaster single-stage press set up solely for 16-gauge loading sits in one corner of the shop, adjusted to one recipe that provides plenty of pop for upland birds and the clay target shooting but that won't shake the that frail little gun apart. The components for those loads are little more expensive, but they are worth it, considering the enjoyment the gun provides.

The author loads thousands of 12-gauge shotshells a year on his RCBS Grand progressive press.

# components

If you're reloading just for plinking or sporting clays you can get away with chilled, dropped (soft) shot; if you're handloading premium target loads you need more expensive magnum (harder) or plated shot or even the non-toxic alternatives such as steel, bismuth or tungsten-alloys.

Magnum lead shot is about 6 percent antimony, compared with 2 percent in chilled shot. There are more pellets in an ounce of magnum lead than chilled or dropped shot, causing a difference in patterning and scores.

Unlike metallic cartridge reloading, each shotshell load carries with it specific and absolute components that must be used. If you can get a good buy on Brand "A" wads as opposed to the specified Brand "B," you can't use them unless you find a load specifying Brand "A"—regardless of what the well-meaning but under-informed sales clerk says about interchangeability of components. If you are bargain hunting, take along a reloading manual to determine if data exists for the components you want to buy.

Savings can obviously be realized by reusing fired hulls. Virtually any target hull can be reloaded, but many use a separate base wad and cheap plastic tube that simply won't reform as consistently, hull-to-hull, as the premium hulls. It's called "memory" and it's part of the reason that premium loads cost so much.

The industry says that the better one-piece hulls like Remington STS, Winchester AA and Federal Gold Medal, can be reloaded about six times. That's actually pretty conservative for target loads. It's not unusual for me to get 15-18 loadings out of a target hull before the crimp starts to get sloppy and the velocity starts to drop due to lessened chamber pressure.

The Remington STS and Nitro Handicap hulls are among the best, but the less-expensive Remington Gun Club hulls are the same configuration and load exactly the same as the more expensive hulls. The plastic is a little cheaper, however, and you won't get quite as many reloads out of a Gun Club hull as you would with an STS or Nitro handicap.

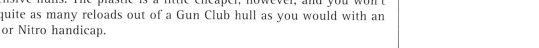

Handloading components include shot, powder, wad, hull and primers.

# handloading slugs

The staggering cost of sabot slugs has sent more than a few serious shooters to the reloading bench, but matching factory ammunition is a difficult, if not impossible situation.

It is impossible in most cases since manufacturers don't sell the components to their sabot slugs. You can build other sabot loads, however.

Part of the difficulty to loading slugs is that the most efficient (in terms of performance and accuracy) form is a rolled crimp. They are a hassle and essentially a one-at-a-time proposition.

The roll crimp is far preferred for slug loads because of that uneven crimping surface provided by the nose of the slug, and because the leaves of a star-crimp will drag on the projectile and effect accuracy.

For roll-crimping, the hull must be secured in a Hull Vise and wad pressure set at 40 pounds to ensure proper wad seating and the evacuation of air between the powder and the wad.

In most cases, the wads were partially sealed into the hull, then the slug was inserted into the sabot, followed by the 40-pounds seating process and completed by crimping.

Roll crimping requires a smooth hull mouth and, as noted previously, you aren't going to get that with a folded crimp hull. The Hull Vise and hull should be positioned on a drill press table and the roll crimp starter (inserted in the drill chuck) slowly lowered into the mouth of the hull. The friction generated from the spinning tool will soften the crimp. Too slow a speed or too fast will likely screw up the process—they say that 300 rpm is ideal but how do you measure that? With a little practice you'll discern the right speed and the correct amount of down pressure.

You can use 3-inch fold-crimped hulls as 2¾-inch slug hulls for roll crimping by trimming a quarter-inch at the bottom of the fold crimp. It's still much better, however, to use roll-crimped production slug hulls to make roll-crimped handloads.

Slug hulls are shorter than the shotshell variety, since the shorter crimp makes it easier to get the slug out of the hull efficiently. You'll also find that if you cut the crimp off longer star-crimped hulls (3½-inchers work well), they can be roll-crimped into 2¾-inch slug hulls quite readily.

Good hulls can easily be reloaded 5-6 times, sometimes as many as 10 times if the loads are not too severe. In fact, we've seen the performance of handloads that used commercial slug hulls get demonstrably better after 2-3 loadings of a particular hull, sometimes dropping the standard deviation to less than 5 feet per second. The plastic in the hulls is losing resiliency and is conforming to the specific dimensions of that shotgun chamber.

They are fire-formed like rifle brass, which expands to precisely fit a particular gun's chamber. But I suspect that another factor of the repeated firings has more import than chamber fit. The slug's crimp is critical to performance and after a couple of loadings and firings the crimp fold will lose its stiffness and open with less resistance upon ignition. Sort of like breaking in a new pair or shoes.

There is obviously a limit to the life of a reloading hull and each should be inspected closely after each firing. Check for interior damage from the powder burn and exterior flaws made by an ejector arm or maybe being crushed underfoot. Also check the basewad. It should be there, obviously, tight and not missing any chunks. Hull shape-up tools are great for inserting and working around the crimp area, relaxing the folds and giving you—or the loader—more room to work with.

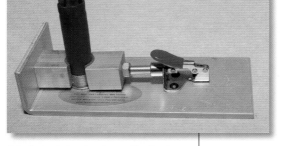

A hull vise is handy when roll-crimping handloaded slugs.

# follow the recipe exactly

Even with slugs, every load takes a specific primer. Substituting one primer for another can diminish or exaggerate performance and almost certainly will alter interior ballistics, which ain't good.

Powders are tailored to load objectives. Slug weight, velocity goals and expected air temperatures are factors when selecting a powder. Cold-temperature slugs and lighter slugs will require faster burning powders for consistent burns. Use a slow-burning powder to tweak a light slug to high velocity only when the conditions are acceptable.

Sealing wads will differ with the various slug and powder combinations. In many cases, conventional cushioned shotcup wads came be used as sabots for rifled barrel loads. Whatever wad you use must seal the gases behind the slug in order to provide consistency.

If you're using a fold crimp, it must be pushed open from the exact center or the slug will enter the barrel tilted. Depending on the style of the slug, it may be difficult to align the nose perfectly every time, which is why overshot wads are needed. It brings the point of force off the outside edge rather than the slug nose.

Some loads, particularly those loaded for smoothbores, require Teflon wrappers to be wrapped around the slug to make the projectile conform more tightly to the barrel. They seem to improve accuracy and reduce deformation of the slug.

Always take into consideration the air temperature when you will be shooting the slugs. Powder loses energy as the air gets colder. All lose a percentage but not at a fixed variable. Each powder type and burn rate is different.

If you are loading at 70 degrees but are looking for performance at 30 degrees, it obviously must be loaded slightly hotter. Fast-burning powders lose less energy with falling temperatures, slow-burning powders lose more, probably because the pressure curve is spread out more and the energy delivered over a longer period of time. If that pressure is not maintained, because of energy loss during cold temperatures, the burning cycle is hampered and consistency and energy is lost.

Low chamber pressure and an ungodly amount of free bore make consistent slug accuracy problematical. When you think about it, you have to wonder why today's slugs shoot as well as they do.

Consider the chamber fit. A 2¾-inch slug actually unfolds to about 2⅝ inches. In a 3-inch chamber, which is what you find in 99 percent of all commercial slug guns, that means a ⅜-inch jump from the .809-inch diameter chamber to the throat of the .729-diameter (.718 in a rifled bore) barrel. If you have a 3½-inch chamber, that's ⅞-inch of freebore!

Imagine that scenario in a rifle.

That's the case with Foster-style or short slugs. Actually, the rear of sabot and attached-wad slugs is still in the hull or very shortly removed from the same, which means it's evenly supported when the nose of the slug reaches the throat of a 3-inch chamber. But in a 3½-inch chamber it's pretty much a leap of faith.

A roll-crimping tool.

*Below:* Slugs for handloaders: (left to right) Aquila finned slug, the BPI Dangerous Game slug, a typical 12-gauge round ball.

*At bottom:* More slugs for handloaders: Gualandi slug and Lyman slug.

# what's available

Ballistic Products, Inc. of Minnesota is absolutely the premier source for slug and/or buckshot handloading components, supplies, manuals, molds, powder, primers, loading tools and virtually anything else the handloader would need or want. They've got plenty of stuff you won't find anywhere else.

Precision Reloading of Connecticut is also a leading shotshell component company and recently entered into the shotgun slug business, marketing, among others, the Lyman and Sabot Technologies' HammerHead slugs.

Today there are still dozens of slug designs available to handloaders

## reloading is not for everyone

Let's understand right up front that reloading is not for everyone. If you must smoke, have distractions nearby, are naturally careless or daring—or if you're the type who doesn't read directions, you are much better off buying your loads at WalMart.

A mature, sensible approach is essential. If you understand and have no problem with the fact that components are not interchangeable and that the reloading process must be conducted with extreme care, thought and precision, you are a candidate for reloading.

It's best to use unibody (one-piece) hulls like Winchester AA, Federal Gold Medal or Remington STS because of their quality, simplicity and because you won't have to add a basewad.

that are sufficiently weird to keep major manufacturers from loading them but that still fill myriad shooting niches and appetites.

Lightfield Hybreds, Barnes Expander SGS, Gualandi and Chris Young's Collett Cup slugs—all of which are also loaded commercially—are available as projectiles through BPI.

The Italian-made Gualandi attached-wad slug, which is loaded commercially by a couple of companies, is available in several sizes through BPI, as is the similarly designed .735-diameter, $1^3/8$-ounce Thunderbolt.

BPI is also an outlet for the one-ounce .735-diameter 12-gauge Mexican-made Aquila (AQ) slugs, which feature nylon gear-like fins that advertising claims imparts a stabilizing rotation.

You can get cast round balls in diameters of .690 (487 grains) and .715 (550 grains) that fit inside conventional shotcups like sabots.

BPI markets a frangible Foster-style slug called the Defender in 10 gauge (.660 diameter, 1.5 ounce) and 20 (.615 diameter, $^7/8$ ounce) and something called an Improved Foster, which is essentially a big wadcutter design with a polished nose that supposedly reduces drag. They are available in 10, 12 and 28 gauge.

Another small-gauge specialty is the Light Game Slug, an attached wad design that comes in 28 gauge (.505 diameter, 183 grains) and .410 (.375 diameter, 93 grains). Lyman offers an hour-glass shaped slug for handloaders and also sells molds for it. Lee also makes a slug mold.

Precision Reloading offers specific recipes for the Sabot Technologies HammerHead—a one-ounce non-discarding sabot slug similar to the Lightfield Commander design. The heavy sabot is a major advantage in that it gives the load a very high ballistic coefficient and can be loaded with a variety of slugs (lead, tungsten, copper, etc.) that make it appealing to special-use applications such as piercing armor, doors or windshields.

# loading equipment

Your biggest cash outlay will be the purchase of loading equipment, but that cost can be amortized over years of shooting. If you just want to try shotshell reloading to see if you like it, many metallic cartridge reloading presses can be fitted to load shotshells. Actually, you can get a single-stage (one shell at a time), shotgun-specific loader for about $50 that is an excellent beginning tool, or a better one for less than $150 that could last a lifetime.

There are anal folks who will sit down and amortize the price of reloading equipment at 3 cents per round and tell you how long it will take to "pay for" that equipment

My RCBS Grand progressive (works like an assembly line) press—the cleanest-operating, most efficient shotshell press I've ever encountered—costs more than $600, but I'm counting on a lifetime of use.

In reality, handloaders don't actually save money. The simply reinvest all of their savings into shooting more often. And there's definitely something to be said for that.

# reloading

The actual process of loading shotshells is pretty straightforward. What follows is the step-by-step process on a single-stage, non-progressive press, the simplest available. This type of press loads one shell at a time, the shell manually moved from die station to die station until all the operations have been performed.

The case body and metal head is full-length resized; the fired primer removed (decapping); a new primer seated (priming); the powder charge dropped; the wad seated; shot charge dropped; the crimp started and the final crimp applied. While there may be operational differences among presses, they are likely minor and will be covered in the instructional manual that comes with each press.

Progressive presses perform all of the same functions, in the same relative order, as those outlined in the preceding paragraph, but the functions are performed on each pull of the lever at different stations on different hulls.

The loading process in a progressive press starts with the tool shell plate empty. You insert a case, perform the first step, advance the shell plate, insert a second case, perform two operations, and so on, until the press has six cases in the shell plate—one positioned at each station. After that you will need to simply keep feeding cases and components in order to obtain a fully loaded round for each down-up stroke of the press handle.

The loading process begins at the left front of the tool, progresses counter-clockwise, and the finished round is removed from the 9 o'clock position.

Even modest efforts on most non-progressive presses will yield the reloader 50-60 rounds per hour. The video that comes with the RCBS Grand claims that you can load 600 rounds an hour, but that's a bit of an exaggeration. If you had a third hand, and an assistant, you couldn't do it.

With the loader perfectly adjusted and full, and dropping loaded shells into a bucket rather than boxing them, I can load a case (250 shells) in an hour on a good day. And that's plenty.

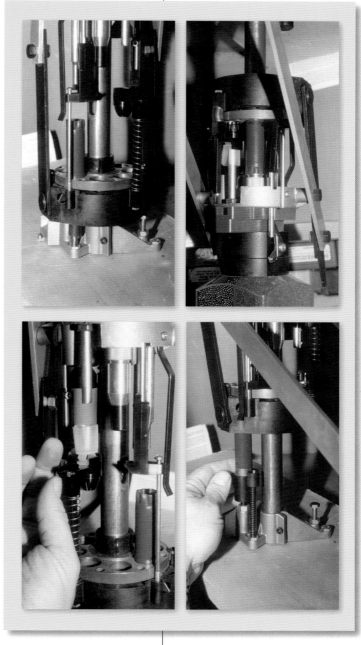

*Top Left:* The hull is decapped in the first station, and capped in the second. *Right:* After powder is dispensed, the hull is inserted in the wad station.

*Bottom Left:* Then it's on to the shot-loading station. *Right:* And finally to the crimping stations.

# Turkey Hunting

A good turkey load has a dense core pattern that can be centered on the bird's head and neck.

The gobbler is answering every cluck and yelp I throw his way, but he's clearly not interested—not with three more corporeal ladies accompanying him toward the roosting area higher in the pine-shrouded draw.

Guide Roger Dubs and I have been chasing this peripatetic band of Merriam's up and down the deep cut ravines of Wyoming's Black Hills country for a couple of hours and are by now resolved to the gobbler's indifference. But we're burning daylight on the next to last day of the hunt and a storm front is approaching.

Bushwhack time. It may well be our last chance, so I slip into the Ponderosa pine tree line above the birds as they feed their way up the draw.

Within minutes they wander into view, crossing the high park. The laser rangefinder reads 58 yards to the gobbler and it's clear that he isn't coming any closer, despite my come-hither ministrations.

Understand that I am adamantly opposed to long range shots at turkeys. Experience has shown 40 yards to be extreme range, even for an veteran shooter with a good pattern. Any success beyond that falls more heavily into the realm of luck than ballistic performance. In more than 20 years of turkey hunting I can count on one hand the number of shots I've taken longer than that—and each was either a miscalculation of yardage or a special circumstance.

Today it's special circumstance. I've done exhaustive pattern testing with this gun, choke and load and know its potential at this distance. Plus the load is tungsten, which means the pellets will carry plenty of energy at the distance.

I yelp twice, then line up the Remington 870 SPT-TH's TruGlo fiber optic sights with the gobbler's red head, squeezing the trigger just as he extends his neck to answer with a gobble.

BOOM!

Recovering from recoil, I see the bird flopping away the last few seconds of life, having stepped in front of a snarling swarm of Hevi-Shot No. 6 pellets.

"I figured we were done for sure," Roger says, wandering down from his perch 40 yards farther up the hill. "I thought he was too far to shoot."

"It was," I answered, gathering my gear and heading to retrieve the bird.

"Too far" has always been relative, but today's high-tech tungsten-

*Next page:*
Today's turkey guns are deadly virtually as far as they will pattern well and loads are effective past 50 yards.

A good turkey hunter should know the size of his pattern at various ranges.

alloy turkey loads really stretch the envelope. I debated long and hard over the ethics of including the yardage figure in this story. And I am by no means advising that anyone shoot such a distance without a thorough knowledge of the load's pattern and energy—and plenty of experience shooting it.

But today's tungsten turkey and waterfowl loads by Remington (Wingmaster HD), Winchester (Xtended Range), Federal (Mag-Shok Heavyweight) and Environ-Metal (Hevi-13, et al), if centered on the target, can pattern tight enough and will kill beyond 50 yards.

They represent the latest developments in the commercial battle for turkey hunters' attention and retail dollar. Twenty years ago they started marketing copper- and nickel-plated shot to tighten patterns for turkey guns, then it was the booming 2-ounce load, then the 2½-ouncer for 3½-inch chambers. When it was widely written that the 2-ounce loads were too slow, first Winchester, then Federal and Remington stepped in with lighter loads and new wads that were much faster and patterned better.

Then Hevi-Shot introduced a tungsten alloy shot that carried its energy much farther than lead, and the newest chapter of "The Ultimate Turkey Load" started.

Granted, tungsten loads have been around a while. The key to the success of the newest versions is the quality of their patterns. Tungsten is an element that is denser and therefore heavier than lead, but is much, much harder and far less malleable.

To be used in ordnance, it must be mixed with something softer. Iron, tin, nickel, copper and various polymers have been used with varying degrees of success in waterfowl loads by Federal, Kent and EnvironMetal.

Federal Cartridge actually made the first major moves with tungsten-iron and later tungsten-polymer non-toxic loads for waterfowl in the 1990s. Kent Cartridge followed with tungsten-tin alloy loads. Early tungsten-based loads were difficult to pattern and the payloads had to be smaller than lead because of the thick wads required to protect barrels from the extremely hard pellets. The saving grace was that the denser, heavier tungsten-alloy pellets carried their energy so much farther that smaller shot sizes matched the effectiveness of large lead pellets.

The difference between the new loads and comparably sized lead pellets varies from 25 to nearly 35 percent, meaning, for example, that tungsten-alloy No. 6 shot pretty much outstrips lead No. 4 in energy.

Metallurgist Darryl Amick came up with the answer to the patterning problem in the form of Hevi-Shot in the late 1990s but at first couldn't convince any major manufacturers to load his unique tungsten-nickel load, despite its properties. Amick's Oregon-based Environ-Metal. Inc. eventually hired specialty loader Jay Menefee of Georgia to load shells under the Hevi-Shot label, and my first experience with the wonder alloy came when Jay called to suggest that I try the hot new loads in the goose season in the late stages of the 20th Century.

They were remarkable. Being old enough to have hunted waterfowl with lead before it became a 4-letter word to environmentalists, Hevi-Shot's effectiveness and range brought back fond memories. It also patterned much better than previous tungsten alloys I'd tested.

When Remington started loading and marketing Hevi-Shot in 2002, it retired my favorite lead turkey loads. It also retired my .660-diameter turkey choke. I found a choke diameter of .675 handled Hevi-Shot best for my purposes. That's the tube that was in the 870 in the opening scenario.

Remington's Hevi-Shot had been such a retail home run in the turkey market that it was only natural that Federal and Winchester would react. But it took quite a bit of research and development before they had answers.

Federal's Heavyweight is billed as a "proprietary tungsten alloy" and is virtually an identical tungsten-iron blend to the company's (then under different ownership and guidance) original mid-1990s shot. It is still very heavy; 35 percent denser than lead, but a totally different manufacturing process from Asia—and Federal's innovative Flitecontrol wad—have turned the load into a silk purse, so to speak.

The new wad is actually an inverted version of a conventional shot cup and Federal Cartridge's parent company's (ATK) background in advanced weapons and space systems played no small part in its development.

Where standard shot cups have long petals that peel back from the front and "blossom" quickly to free the charge, the Flitecontrol wads feature solid tubes at the leading edge with short rear petals. These are flared by expanding gases and act like braking flaps on an airplane wing. As a result the wad stays with the charge longer and gradually releases the pellets in a uniform and denser manner.

The denser patterns and industry-leading density make for a remarkably effective turkey load. I scored a dead-in-its-tracks hit on a big Rio Grande gobbler in Texas when he hung up on the far side of a barbed wire fence at 51 yards shortly before the Wyoming hunt featured in the opening scenario. The load's patterns in the .675 Remington Hevi-Shot choke tube at 40 yards left no doubt in my mind as to its potential lethality over 50.

Winchester's new Xtended Range load is a veritable twin of Hevi-Shot at 10 percent heavier than lead. Winchester's marketing never mentions its tungsten (with copper-nickel-iron) makeup, probably to avoid the appearance of jumping on the tungsten bandwagon. Big Red makes a big deal out of the roundness of the Xtended Range pellets, which can be

This pattern was fired using an Ithaca Model 87 with a Winchester 2-oz, No. 5 shell.

perceived as a comparison to Hevi-Shot's random-shaped pellets.

It is by far the softest and most versatile patterning load among new ones, achieving absolutely deadly patterns well beyond 40 yards with a Hunters Specialties Undertaker tube in a Thompson Center Encore 12-gauge shotgun on a hunt this spring in Colorado. Remarkably, it also patterned well out of my .660 Rhino tube in a 24-inch backbored Ithaca Model 37 barrel in a testing session on my home range.

Taking aim at a turkey early in the morning.

Hevi-13 is Environ-Metal's latest concoction, probably introduced to keep stride with other new loads. Hevi-13 is slightly more than 20 percent heavier than lead, and about 8 percent heavier than Remington Hevi-Shot, placing its density between the Federal and Winchester loads.

The Environ-Metal engineers achieved this by increasing the percentage of tungsten in the load, and off-setting the resultant hardness with a unique coating of molybdenum disulfide—which, if I'm not mistaken, is the stuff with which Winchester coats its FailSafe rifle ammunition. The coating makes the irregularly-shaped Hevi-13 pellets slicker and more friendly toward one another in their passage down the barrel and the subsequent rush for position in the shot string.

# preparation

I did exhaustive pattern testing with all four tungsten-alloy choices, before and after hunts where I killed three birds with the Federal, Remington and Winchester brands. Range testing was conducted on Birchwood Casey Shoot-N-C 10-inch black-faced targets at various yardages and later at the company's turkey head targets, using a .695 Hunters Specialties Undertaker tube, a .660 Rhino tube, a .683 Hastings tube and Remington's .675 Hevi-Shot tube. Each was shot through in the aforementioned Remington 870 SPS-TH (thumbhole), Ithaca M37 and Thompson Center Encore shotguns.

I tried to level the platform by testing all 3-inch versions with No. 6 shot, but it was still pretty much an apples-and-oranges comparison. Each load had different amounts of pellets in the hull, different velocities and hardness. Each barrel also had a different internal diameter, and thus different comparative constriction with the choke.

The Winchester Xtended Range load worked fairly well with all the constrictions but, strangely, showed its best (and virtually identical) performance through the .660 Rhino and the .695 HS Strut Undertaker choke tubes—the tightest and most open of the testing tubes.

But the 1¾-ounce Winchester load simply had more pellets in the hull since its shot is softer, allowing a thinner walled shotcup to be used. Hevi-Shot, Heavyweight and Hevi-13 all had 1⅝ ounce payloads.

Remington Hevi-Shot, Hevi-13 and Winchester Xtended Range all posted velocities of 1,225 feet per second at the muzzle while the smaller Federal Heavyweight load was at 1,300 fps.

Xtended Range consistently put the most pellets in any pattern, although Federal Heavyweight was better on some targets with some chokes, and was always very close. The Federal load did not shoot well out of ported choke tubes, throwing very inconsistent patterns. My guess is that the ports somehow compromised the Flitecontrol wad's flaps, damaging its ability to manage the payload.

The Federal, Remington Hevi-Shot and Environ-Metal Hevi-13 loads, being much harder and with fewer pellets in the hull, all liked the .675 constriction best.

Citing the number of holes in various patterns here would be tedious and meaningless. The numbers vary shot-to-shot, even with the same load, and the patterns achieved with any of my chokes and guns would differ from yours simply because of the difference in barrel interior diameters and how they relate to the various choke tube diameters.

The bottom line is that the tungsten-alloy loads are deadlier at longer

The only means of selecting the right turkey load for your gun is to do your research at the range.

ranges than their lead counterparts, but only if the shooter finds the optimum choke constriction for the specific load and demonstrates the ability to put the pattern in the right spot.

## choosing the right load

Turkey hunting is obviously a special application for a shotgun. It's one of the only instances where a scattergun is aimed like a rifle rather than pointed and swung.

The whole idea is to put an extremely dense pattern on a standing bird's vital head and neck area. That's where the aiming comes in. And the quality of that pattern is the bottom line in the whole turkey hunting formula, regardless of what shotgun, choke or load you use.

The most effective turkey gun and load combination is the one that most consistently centers the dense core of its pattern right in the bird's computer room. Hit a turkey in the head and neck with 20-30 pellets and it doesn't matter if they were made of lead or tungsten, if they were flying at 1,300 feet per second or 800, if they were fired from a 10-gauge or a .410.

It is, afterall, not about the size of the dog in the fight, but rather about the fight in the dog. It may be common sense; but there's so much hype about turkey guns and loads out there that the basic truth is somehow lost.

## big bore best?

Probably the most common fallacy among turkey hunters is that the biggest bores and biggest loads are best. They are the most powerful, afterall, and they shoot the farthest.

Well, that's not actually correct. A big bore does have a ballistic advantage, but their individual pellets don't hit any harder than those of equal size in lesser gauges, and they don't carry any farther.

Identical pellets fired at the same velocity will travel the same distance with the same energy and trajectory. If your 20-gauge will put several pellets in a turkey's head and neck at 40 yards, it's just as effective as a 12- or 10-gauge that prints the same number of pellets there.

Yeah, but pellets from a bigger gauge will give you a bigger pattern.

A 10-gauge pattern may be a fraction larger than one from a comparably choked 20-gauge, but the size difference is negligible. Believe it or not, 20-, 12- and 10-gauge patterns, given the same choke constriction, will be virtually the same diameter at any given range.

There is, however, an obvious ballistic advantage to larger gauges. That's because in a scattergun the energy is a cumulative effect of how many pellets hit the target. There are simply more pellets in a larger gauge hull and therefore more pellets in the pattern—giving the bigger gauge loads more energy.

A 10-gauge load doesn't fly any farther than a .410's, but there are so many more pellets that when the respective patterns deteriorate at long range, there are still more pellets flying together in the big-bore's pattern than in the smaller bore's.

Yes, for ballistic reasons bigger is generally better. But ballistic superiority isn't the only consideration when choosing a load for your shotgun.

# importance of patterning

Let's start out with the basic premise that any gauge shotgun, with any load, is sufficient to turn out the lights on a turkey. Granted, with smaller gauges the bird must be must closer for the load to be effective. Basically, the larger the gauge the more efficient it is for clean, reliable kills at longer distances.

As noted, you can make whatever gauge gun you're shooting more effective simply by finding a load and a choke constriction that puts the most possible pellets in the center of the pattern—not necessarily the most holes in the paper but rather the most in the head and neck area. I've seen some custom-choked 20s that would outperform virtually all factory-choked 12s at equal ranges.

That means, of course, that tighter and denser means more than bigger and higher pellet count. If all those extra pellets don't hit what you're aiming at, what are they worth?

Okay, hopefully we've established that the biggest load isn't necessarily the best. How do you determine which is best?

My suggestion is to narrow down the field through research (friends, magazines, store clerks, etc.) and take a select variety of loads to the practice range. Consider 2¾ and 3-inch, and even 3½-inchers if you have to. Also consider 2-ounce and faster 1¾ ouncers, or the 2½-ouncers from the 3½-inch guns. Then consider pellet size and makeup—plated lead, tungsten-alloy, whatever.

Start shooting at 15 yards at a large (at least 40x40 inches) piece of paper. Shoot from a bench if possible and aim at a dot in the center, using any load.

A turkey load is only effective if it patterns tightly.

This exercise tells you where the gun shoots in relation to point of aim. Many guns shoot slightly off-center—some shoot a lot off-center. If your gun doesn't center the pattern exactly where you put the bead you might consider using adjustable sights or a scope that can be adjusted to compensate.

Once that's been established, move back to 25 yards and shoot each load from the bench or rested position at large sheets of paper. Remember that patterning a turkey gun is much different than patterning a gun for wingshooting. Turkey hunters don't necessarily need a nice, round, clean pattern with the shot evenly dispersed. They want a tight pattern that can be ragged at the edges but it must have a very dense core.

When the best patterning loads are determined, walk away from the bench and switch patterns. Using turkey head patterns that are available from a variety of manufacturers, shoot each at a clean target at a variety of ranges. Shooting from a sitting position like you would use in the woods, shoot first at 10 yards, then 15, then 20, 25, 30, 35 and 40.

Note how the pattern changes with yardage. Does it remain dense? How many pellets are striking the head and neck area? At what yardage does the best pattern begin to deteriorate?

This simple exercise will not only tell you which load is best for your gun but will also tell you the size of your pattern at specific ranges—a real aid if a bird steps into a small opening 40 yards away or surprises you by popping up at 12 yards.

### what is "too much?"

Nineteenth century British gun builder William Greener, in his Rule of Ninety-Six, calculated that a shotgun should be 96 times heavier than the weight of the shot charge it fires in order to ensure good patterns.

Under this rule, a shotgun firing a one ounce shot charge should weigh six pounds. An ounce and an eighth load is better suited for a 6¾-pound gun; 7½ pound guns are needed for 1¼-ounce loads. Greener's rule is generally accepted as gospel—meaning today's loads are out of whack.

"What do you expect?" said one outspoken expert in the shotgun ammunition field. "You're shoving what is essentially an 8-gauge load down a 12-gauge barrel. That's a lot of pressure that has to go somewhere." Recoil is definitely a consideration with the ultimate big bore turkey guns.

Consider that the average 2-ounce, 3-inch 12-gauge load—the most popular load sold—shoves the butt of a 7-pound pump gun into your shoulder at 19.265 feet per second for a measured recoil of 43 foot pounds. Most of you will be able to coordinate these figures with experience and know that 3-inch turkey loads certainly get your attention at ignition. By comparison the Barnes Ballistic Program shows that the renowned hard-kicking .375 H&H magnum rifle loaded with its optimum 270-grain hunting load only develops 39.5 foot pounds of recoil.

Now folks, let's consider the big boys. The 3½-inch turkey load in the 7-pound, 12-ounce Mossberg 835 pump develops a whopping 60.3 foot pounds of recoil, hitting your shoulder at a speed of 22.31 feet per second. For comparison that's 6 foot pounds more than a .416 Remington Magnum with a 700-grain bullet—the gun's suggested load for elephants!

The 10-gauge, given its roomier bore and hull and greater gun heft but identical-sized load, is far less punishing despite a 60 fps velocity advantage over the stoked-to-the-limit 3½-inch 12-gauge. A 2¼-ounce 10-gauge load fired from my 11-pound Ithaca Mag-10 develops 48.7 foot pounds of recoil at a speed of 16.88 feet per second. That's no love pat but is considerably less formidable than the long 12.

Americans love muscle and the 10-gauge and 3½-inch 12s are the brutes of the shotgun set. The mentality is that bigger is stronger and better. But just as in sports bigger usually means slower—and velocity is a key ingredient in a load's energy at impact.

The initial shots of a patterning session should be done from a solid rest to determine if the gun shoots where it's aimed.

The advantage to the bigger gauges is more room for payload and propellant. They don't shoot any farther than small bores—there's just more pellets in the big bore string when it reaches the longer distances.

But velocity is still a major factor.

The 3½-inch 12 gauge is, more accurately, a modern substitute for the 10-gauge, which itself still maintains a presence among older turkey hunters. Both guns shoot essentially the same 2¼-ounce load of Nos. 4,5, or 6 shot in Remington, Federal, Winchester and Kent loadings but the bigger bore's heft helps absorb some of the felt recoil.

The 3½-inch chambered Mossberg 835 Ultra-Mag weighs 7 pounds 12 ounces and quakes mightily when that "8-gauge load" is forced down the 1¼-inch diameter barrel. The 9-pound Browning BPS is only marginally gentler when handling the 3½-inch loads.

When all the information is weighed and tallied the figures show that yes, the 2¼-ounce payloads from 3½-inch 12- and 10-gauge guns are indeed the biggest, baddest loads available for turkey hunting.

But because of their makeup, it's far more difficult to get an effective pattern with them than it is with a much smaller and faster conventional load.

The question is, if the extra pellets are largely wasted and the recoil is prohibitive, where is the advantage?

In today's turkey woods the bird is outmatched by shotgun technology.

# Waterfowl Hunting

Waterfowl guns, then and now: The Marlin 55 Goose Gun has a 36-inch barrel; the Ithaca Mag-10 was the first 10-gauge autoloader and the Inertia-driven Benelli Super Black Eagle II.

*Next page:*
Ready for the next shot. Modern waterfowl hunters have a wide selection of non-lead shot from which to choose.

Those of us who are old enough to have hunted waterfowl with lead shot can appreciate the difference between then and now.

Although it's long been a munitions designer's dream metal, lead's poisonous qualities began manifesting themselves in the outdoors years ago and in short order it became a 4-letter word to environmentalists.

As a result, waterfowl hunting, for the last couple of decades, has been all about doing the right thing—getting the lead out.

A controversial biological study conducted by the U.S. Fish and Wildlife Service in 1957 alleged significant waterfowl mortality from lead poisoning caused by ingesting spent lead pellets while feeding. Then we were told that countless raptors were similarly dying after feeding on the carcasses of lead-poisoned ducks!

The feds' answer was to outlaw the use of lead shot for waterfowl, and eventually for all shooting. Lead shot was prohibited on refuges and other areas starting in the 1980s and was phased out of American waterfowl hunting altogether in 1991. Canada followed suit in 1996.

The EPA is now busy getting lead out of fishing (jigs and sinkers) and surveying lead contamination on the grounds of shooting ranges and hunting preserves across the country. The non-toxic day has dawned and waterfowlers were the test pilots for the rest of the shooting-hunting industry.

Getting the lead out of waterfowl hunting meant finding a suitable alternative. Lead's replacement had to be non-toxic to ducks to please the feds. But it confounded ballisticians, not to mention hunters, for years.

Hopefully the newest tungsten-alloy exotics from Hevi-Shot, Winchester (Xtended Range) and Federal Heavyweight will be the answer. But even that is changing as Hevi-Shot dissolved its partnership with Remington in 2005 and the latter came up with its own new non-toxic tungsten-alloy blend the next year.

Regardless, the tungsten-alloy loads have ended my search, for the time being. But more on that later.

# started with steel

Steel was the first alternative. Ballistically steelshot compared to lead like paperwads did to ball bearings. It was more expensive and far less dense, which meant it lost energy far quicker than lead. The pellets also didn't deform when they hit something, which ain't good.

Steel threw nice, neat, clean patterns because the pellets didn't deform, but the shorter shot string and shorter effective range meant a legion of waterfowl hunters had to learn to shoot all over again.

Those hard little pellets would score barrels, swell choke tubes to the point that you couldn't remove them and rip through ducks and geese without leaving the quickly fatal wound channels or drag feathers into the wounds like deformed lead pellets did.

Despite all these charming qualities, steel is, decades later, the overwhelming choice of serious waterfowlers. That should tell you what the subsequent non-toxic loads must have been like to make steel look so good.

Granted, steelshot has been improved mightily over the last couple of decades. New manufacturing processes for shot; improved wad designs and cleaner-burning powders have made it very effective at limited ranges. Dedicated waterfowlers adjusted and some accepted the inevitable; and today thousands of young hunters have never used anything else.

To be honest, today's waxed, copper-plated steel or zinc-galvanized (to prevent rusting and choke damage) buffered loads are very effective on geese out to 40 yards in most shot sizes — which should be sufficient for any hunter. And high-velocity loads from Federal and Winchester even push that envelope farther.

But probably the one trait of steel shot that has kept it more popular than the alternatives is its price point.

The U.S. Fish & Wildlife Service has approved steel and ultra-expensive bismuth-tin and a variety of tungsten alloys for waterfowl hunting. Despite this, an industry that has looked at everything from depleted uranium to molybeum and varied polymers to polysyllabic entities only a metallurgist could love is still seeking the ultimate non-toxic shot.

For a while it looked like the tungsten-polymers were the answer, but now the smart money is on Hevi-Shot and its tungsten-alloy brethren.

Awaiting a flight of ducks in a blind on Maryland's Eastern Shore.

# selecting chokes

In the formative years of steel shot's use for waterfowl hunting the rule of thumb was to open chokes at least one constriction more for steel than you did for lead. Steel pellets were much harder and therefore less susceptible to deformation than lead and thus threw a tighter pattern without as much constriction.

But as technology advanced in both steel shot loadings and choke tubes, that thinking has changed a bit. It's not so simple any more.

Shooters are finding that a modified choke no longer throws steel loads in patterns that fit within full-choke parameters like they once did. At least not in the smaller sizes, like No. 2s through 6s or 8s. Today's smaller pellets spread well with open chokes but through modified chokes they pretty much shoot patterns that fit within conventional modified parameters.

Large steel shot, however, and I'm talking No. 1s and BBs and even F-shot, will quite often throw a full-choke pattern through a modified choke. Of course it will vary with chamber size, barrel and the brand of chokes you use, but generally speaking, steel shot patterning is changing.

Tungsten-iron patterned much like steel (much denser patterns) but subsequent exotics such as bismuth-tin, tungsten-polymer, tungsten-matrix and the new tungsten-alloy exotics by Hevi-Shot, Federal and Winchester exhibit patterning characteristics much like lead loads.

When I first handled Hevi-Shot I nearly dismissed it as another over-hyped, over-priced, non-toxic shotshell. The first hull I opened looked like junk—the pellets were spherical and irregularly shaped rather than round. How would that ever pattern efficiently?

The Winchester Super-X2 autoloader is a virtual twin to the Browning Gold.

The Federal Heavyweight and Winchester Xtended Range loads are slightly different alloys than Hevi-Shot and are made by a totally different process that leaves the pellets round. But the killing effect among the three is very similar.

Federal Heavyweight is, in fact, identical in composition to the company's disappointing tungsten-iron loads, but is manufactured by a totally different process and, with the revolutionary new Flitecontrol wad, patterns as well as anything on the market.

The density of the remarkable tungsten-alloy does it. Mass is the over-riding factor in good shotshell patterns. Jay Menefee of Polywad Company, who loaded Hevi-Shot for the Environ-Metal Company before Remington picked up the banner in 2001, compares it to the phenomenon of a mis-shapen rock flying straighter than a perfectly round ping pong ball.

They are heavier (relative to their size) than any civilian available shotshell pellets and thus can carry farther and hit harder (less air resistance to small, heavy pellets that can maintain energy comparable to much larger pellets of lighter material). They are heavier than lead (specific density of 11.8 vs. 11.2 for pure lead), and they're heavier still than lead pellets containing lightweight antimony.

# bismuth, the next non-toxic

In the early 1990s bismuth replaced steel, on the drawing boards at least, as a front-runner among the lead-replacement wannabes.

Before that a Canadian ballistician was designing bismuth-alloy mixes and loads and eventually enlisted a couple of British companies to load them. With U.S. waterfowlers frowning at steel, American developers became interested and the Bismuth Cartridge Company of Dallas, Texas, was formed. It too enlisted the British to assemble the early loadings.

Bismuth Cartridge was a very small firm, lacking the squads of lawyers and researchers needed to influence the U.S. Fish & Wildlife Service. Thus Bismuth's acceptance by USFWS was delayed until 1995.

When Federal Cartridge Company introduced its Premium tungsten-iron loads in 1996 munitions giant Winchester-Olin quickly formed an alliance with Bismuth Cartridge (announced in January 1997) to offset its competitors' potential advantage in the waterfowl market. The partnership was dissolved in 2000.

So what is bismuth? Well, the scholarly will note that it is an inert elemental metal that sits squarely between lead (Pb) and polonium (Po) in the Periodic Table of Elements. It has a specific gravity very close (91 percent) to that of lead and is about 14 percent lighter. Like steel, it's damned hard but malleable enough (when mixed with 3-4 percent tin) to be molded into round pellets.

Trivia buffs will note that bismuth is the chief ingredient in the timeless upset stomach remedy Pepto-Bismol.

Several years ago we patterned some early-generation bismuth loads and found that the pellets actually shattered upon setback on occasion. Reprising that field testing role in the mid-1990s, however, we saw very little indication of shattering in the then newly buffered Bismuth Cartridge loadings. But when we shot through some skinned chicken carcasses some of the bismuth pellets left very small slivers in the flesh.

Regardless of its popularity, bismuth has not and will not flood the market. There simply isn't very much of the stuff available in the few American and South American mines unearthing it.

It should be noted that Winchester then negotiated with Enviro-Metal for exclusive right to market Hevi-Shot but balked at the numbers, which is when Remington stepped in. After several successful years together Remington stepped out in 2006, which leaves tiny Hevi-Shot to its own devices.

# early tungsten loads

The next big breakthrough after bismuth was Federal's tungsten-iron load, which might be more accurately named "improved steel." Given tungsten's extreme hardness, copious amounts of iron must be added in order to soften the alloy sufficiently to die-form and heat-sinter it into pellets. Federal's Premium Tungsten pellets were actually 60 percent iron and 40 percent tungsten.

No sooner had complaints about its extreme hardness begun to ring out than Federal introduced a softer, better performing tungsten-polymer load. Kent Cartridge, a Canadian firm that in 1998 took over the facilities at the financially plagued Activ complex in West Virginia, followed Federal's lead with a virtually identical (in a performance sense) tungsten-matrix (which uses tin in the alloy) load.

"There's not a thing wrong with tungsten-polymer or matrix," noted a renowned load designer and waterfowl hunter, who asked to stay anonymous here since he's looking for work after having served with two of the largest manufacturers. "It's resilient. It deforms well on impact. It drags feathers into the wound channel. It just kills real well."

In fact, the tungsten-polymer or matrix loads virtually mirror lead loads in ballistics, performance and efficiency. The drawback is that in softening the alloy, patterning becomes inconsistent. That's the reasoning behind the development of Federal's duplex tungsten-iron-steel load, which consists of a layer of steel pellets laid over a layer of tungsten-iron pellets.

The theory behind duplex loads is that they will pattern extremely well with the steel helping fill in pattern density at short ranges and the tungsten-iron carrying its energy much farther down range. In my experience, however, while duplex loads look good on a patterning board, cutting the advantages of both pellets by cutting their respective numbers just waters down performance.

The retail prices for all the alternatives, however, may well make waterfowlers find they didn't hate steel as much as they thought they did.

Good steel loads are likely to cost up to 70 cents per shot while bismuth is about $1.90 for each trigger pull and tungsten-polymer or matrix loads are in the $2 per category. Hevi-Shot and its new tungsten-alloy buddies figure to be even more expensive.

The Benelli Super Black Eagle II is the state-of-the-art hunting autoloader and the author's choice as a waterfowl gun.

# tungsten-iron drawbacks

Marketing of the tungsten-iron load touts the fact that it is 94 percent as dense as lead, 32 percent denser than steel and 10 percent denser than bismuth. It is also 30 percent harder than steel, which should throw up a red flag for seasoned observers. I've seen tungsten-iron BBs blow right through 20-gauge galvanized sheet metal at 30 yards—handy if you have to defend yourself against small aircraft but too much zip without deformation to be regularly effective on waterfowl.

Like steel, because of its hardness, tungsten-iron shot should not be fired through double guns or older thin-walled barrels or choke tube systems —areas where bismuth and lead are acceptable. Tungsten-iron patterns tighter than bismuth or lead, much like steel loads, since the hardness of the pellets limits deformity at setback or through chokes. The tungsten-iron pellets are so hard that a very thick plastic wad must be employed to protect barrel walls. The wad takes up more room in the hull than do wads in the other loads, leaving less space for pellets.

# newest tungsten loads

Despite the marketing blitz that put Federal Premium Tungsten-iron at the forefront of high-tech legal goose loads, I've always felt that its performance as a hunting load was significantly inferior to that of Winchester-Bismuth or the Federal or Kent tungsten loads despite the higher price tag. Tungsten-iron's potential is also limited by the difficulty of manufacture, because of tungsten's hardness. The tungsten-polymers and matrix and bismuths demonstrated superiority in energy transfer and wound channel size simply make them better killing loads than tungsten-iron. Bismuth approaches lead load performance and the polymer and matrix loads match it while tungsten-iron comes off as a simple improvement over steel.

Meanwhile tungsten-polymer and matrix pellets pattern almost like lead—which is what we're all looking for in a non-toxic alternative—and, like bismuth-tin, can be shot through any gun. They throw a far more forgiving spread than steel or tungsten-iron and exhibit shot-stringing characteristics nearly identical to those of high performance lead loads.

Both the bench and field tests showed that the Federal tungsten-polymer and Kent tungsten-matrix loads were marginal improvements over bismuth. The tungsten off-shoots were virtually identical to each other in ballistics and performance.

Overall, it will take an awfully sensitive hand with a shotgun to notice the performance difference between lead and bismuth-tin or the newer tungsten-polymer and matrix loads. But Hevi-Shot, Remington Wingmaster HD, Federal Heavyweight and Winchester Xtended Range were immediately visible improvements in patterning, and that's what we're looking for in the goose fields.

Tungsten-iron's potential is also limited by the difficulty of manufacture ...

## steel shot pellets per load

| | Steel Shot Sizes | | | | | | | | | |
|---|---|---|---|---|---|---|---|---|---|---|
| Charge (oz) | F | T | BBB | BB | 1 | 2 | 3 | 4 | 5 | 6 |
| 1/2 | 30 | 39 | 46 | 54 | 77 | 94 | 118 | 144 | 186 | 236 |
| 15/16 | 37 | 49 | 58 | 67 | 87 | 117 | 149 | 180 | 230 | 295 |
| 1 | 40 | 52 | 62 | 72 | 103 | 125 | 155 | 189 | 243 | 314 |
| 1 1/8 | 45 | 58 | 70 | 80 | 116 | 141 | 175 | 212 | 274 | 335 |
| 1 1/4 | 50 | 67 | 76 | 89 | 129 | 156 | 194 | 237 | 304 | 394 |
| 1 3/8 | 55 | 73 | 84 | 97 | 141 | 170 | 212 | 360 | 334 | 433 |
| 1 1/2 | 60 | 78 | 93 | 108 | 154 | 187 | 237 | 288 | 364 | 472 |
| 1 5/8 | 62 | 81 | 97 | 112 | 161 | 195 | 247 | 300 | 380 | 492 |
| 1 7/8 | 65 | 84 | 101 | 117 | 167 | 203 | 257 | 312 | 395 | 512 |

A Winchester Super-X2 goes to work in a frosty goose field.

# The Art of Wingshooting

Measuring, swinging and executing a 35-yard crossing shot on a blue-winged teal flying downwind in a gale—while battling blowing rain and bulky parka—has a degree of difficulty equivalent to surfing the Banzai Pipeline on a 2-by-4.

Well, almost. But you get the picture.

If you ascribe to the theory that hitting a pitched ball is the most difficult of all athletic moves, you've obviously never seriously tried shooting a firearm offhand at a flying target.

Granted, hitting a baseball is difficult. And most folks find consistently hitting a golf ball straight and long to be a nearly impossible task. But in my experience—and I played ball at the semi-professional level and had a single-digit handicap in golf—there is no comparison to the difficulty in wingshooting.

Ball fields and golf courses are toddlers' sandboxes in comparison to the sporting clays course or dove field.

Granted, batting, golfing and shooting are intimidating; difficult. All require a modicum of eye-to-hand coordination and physical flexibility.

But wingshooting trumps the others simply because of the space, logistics and equipment needed to participate and the lack of access to interested or qualified instructors. Afterall, a kid can learn to hit with a little instruction from virtually any adult and a batting tee, and a video can teach you a repeatable golf swing in a matter of minutes. But becoming an effective wingshot takes an expert watching over the student's shoulder on a range where clay birds can be thrown with repetitive accuracy. The money, time and travel required to partake of wingshooting instruction really limit the number of applicants.

Instead, most of us learn to shoot without ever learning to shoot; if that makes any sense. Most experienced shooters simply grabbed a gun when they were young and shot it until they were able to hit something consistently—without ever knowing how or why. Many more became discouraged they couldn't hit anything, not knowing how or why, and gave up.

When shooting target games your gun's action should be open whenever you are not shooting.

*Next page:*
Hitting a moving target with a shotgun is among the most difficult movements in sports.

# shooting methods

There are several basic styles of attacking a flying target, and all may be required to successfully navigate a good, varied sporting clays course—or a hectic dove field.

The basic mechanical methods are sustained lead, pull-through and spot shooting. Most instructors today teach the Churchill Method, or other variations of the purely instinctive style.

Sustained lead shooting entails swinging the muzzle a given distance in front of the target and maintaining that distance while shooting until the follow-through is complete. In practice, sustained lead is easy to learn and difficult to apply to a variety of shooting conditions. It is, nevertheless, an excellent method for skeet shooting, where all targets are predictable in speed and angle, day-to-day and field-to-field.

Swing-through or pull-through is the method in which the muzzle is swung from behind the target, traces the flight path of the target, then the load is triggered as the muzzle swings past or ahead of the target. The move must be continued with a follow-through to assure sufficient muzzle speed. This method is more difficult to learn than sustained lead and requires more practice to keep the timing sharp. But it is more versatile and applicable to virtually all forms of shotgun shooting.

All of these versions, plus the Churchill Method-inspired instinctive shooting, require mechanical moves honed by repetition and triggered by subconscious focus on the part of the shooter.

Most good shooters today practice all methods and employ whichever works best for the type of target they are confronted with.

An indoor shooting drill: With a MagLite flashlight in the barrel, practice mounting your gun and tracing the light beam across the ceiling molding. Repeat 10-20 times on a daily basis and your mount will become smooth and natural.

# the dominant eye

Virtually all instructors will start by having students determine their dominant or "master" eye. I say "virtually all" because there is a group out there, including some of my friends, that believes that the dominant eye makes no difference.

I beg to differ, having seen far too many "cross dominant" (left eye-dominant right-handers and vice versa) battle the condition without ever coming close to a target. The cross-dominant person, without correction, will always be looking in a different direction than the gun muzzle is pointed. That is obviously not good.

To combat this, a spot or even a slight smudge can be placed in a strategic spot on the dominant eye's lens of the shooting glasses. The spot draws that eye's attention, making the brain rely on the other eye to track the target.

Contrary to popular belief, the dominant eye is not the stronger but simply the one that focuses first.

Shooting with a mounted gun, which is common in skeet, trap and recreational forms of sporting clays, demands more of the dominant eye—as does the sustained lead or pull-through techniques of shooting. It is less important in instinctive shooting.

## determining dominant eye

There is a simple exercise used to determine one's dominant eye. Look at a distant object, then frame it in a "window" formed by your hands, held palms-out at arm's length.

Now close one eye. If the target object is still visible, the open eye is dominant. If it disappears, you've closed the dominant eye. One variation of this method is to keep both eyes open and slowly draw the interwined hands back toward your face. The framing hands will automatically go to the dominant eye.

Once the dominant eye has been determined, the second step is to learn how to stand while swinging and shooting at a moving target.

Determining the dominant eye.

# focus on the target

Gil and Vicki Ash run Optimal Shooting Performance, a shooting school at Houston's American Shooting Center. They approach shooting from both the mechanical and psychological angles.

Yet their concept is extremely simple: Look at the target. Put the gun where the target is going. Pull the trigger. It's that simple! Anything else you put into the shot just clutters up the mechanics and takes away from your focus (concentration) on the target.

"You read lots of articles and watch lots of videos on swing through, pull away, maintained lead, sustained lead, modified pull away, diminishing maintained swing-stab, etc.," says Gil, who has the inflection and voice tone of evangelical minister. "Although all of these are mechanical techniques, they have more to do with a person's style than anything else.

"Each technique has risks. Some have more than others. But they all have great risk when a shooter's focus is on technique and not on the target. We feel that way too many people get hung up in the trip that the gun is making and they lose sight of where it needs to go.

"The gun must be in front of the bird when the shot is taken. The more time you spend thinking about what the gun is doing the worse you will shoot.

"Instead of focusing on the trip the gun is making, FOCUS on the destination and the trip will take care of itself. You'll hit more targets and have a lot more fun."

Quite simply, if the barrel is moving on the same line and speed as the target, you'll break the bird.

## subconscious focus

You'll hear shooters talk about keeping their minds blank when shooting. They actually try to clear all conscious thoughts and let their subconscious mind find, focus and track the target.

"There is a 3/10 of a second delay from the conscious mind to the hands," explains Gil Ash, whose book *If It Ain't Broke, Fix it!* may be the best book ever written on the subject of wingshooting.

"If your eyes are telling your brain where to be, and if it takes 3/10 of a second to get there, then you will be behind. This game can't be played in the past.

"Look at the front of the target and let the gun get somewhere in the front and pull the trigger. Too much thinking about where the gun is, leads to being behind. Your focus must be completely on the target.

"Be more concerned about your focus on the target and let the mind-body computer do its job."

Many instructors liken this to throwing a ball to another person. You don't think about the mechanics of your arm or body but rather focus on the other guy's glove and let your mind do the guidance.

To understand wingshooting, Ash says you must first understand your visual circle. Within your visual circle you have two types of vision, primary or sharp vision and peripheral vision.

A small flashlight, wrapped with duct tape for a firm fit in the shotgun barrel, is an excellent tool for practicing your gun mount.

Look across the room at a small object, like the corner of a picture frame or a light switch. Although you are focused on the light switch, you are aware of everything else in the room that is in front of you. Your primary vision is focused on the light switch and your peripheral vision sees everything else in the room.

This is your visual circle. Your primary vision (on the light switch) is .02 percent of everything you see. Your peripheral circle is 99.98% of everything you see. Your peripheral circle calculates distance, direction, and speed—that is its job. Your primary circle tells the peripheral circle what object to calculate this data from.

The target always stays in your primary vision. We call this the conscious or input side of the computer. The gun always stays in the peripheral circle. We call this the subconscious or output side of your computer.

When shooting a target you must be consciously focused on the front of the target in order for your subconscious mind to be able to place the gun ahead of where the target is. The reason they say focus on the front is that you obtain target location and line in one simple picture. Because of the size of the pattern and the length of the shot string, there is a tremendous amount of forgiveness with respect to lead.

If and only if the gun and the target are moving in the same direction and speed and the gun is somewhere (within reason) ahead of the bird be precise in focus and sloppy with lead. However, this forgiveness is only in existence when the primary or conscious vision stays on the target.

A major problem for inexperienced shooters is picking up the flight of the target out of the trap, then catching up.

"The eyes must locate the target, then focus on it," said Ash, who teaches 1,500 to 2,000 students annually. "If your eyes are beyond the flight line of the target, and focused on something stationary, they will pick up any movement that they see. In one function, they will immediately go to the object that is moving the fastest in the picture and focus on it.

"This way you are allowing the eyes to give the computer (brain) the correct information and make the correct picture happen."

By placing the index finger along the forearm rather than under it the shooter can get the feel of pointing to the target.

## why bird hunting is different

Experienced bird hunters may have trouble on a clays course for a couple of reasons. First of all, clay targets are continually slowing as they get farther from the trap, while a bird will usually maintain a constant speed.

Secondly, bird hunters have a problem maintaining focus on a clay target. On a live bird the shooter's eyes will naturally go to the fastest moving thing on the bird—the wings. This gives them focus and helps them maintain it.

They also have a head to focus on a live bird. Their eyes can then move to the head of the bird and put the barrel where the bird is going. A lot of hunters and shooters don't realize that if they do not look at the head (or leading edge of the target) that their eyes naturally will go to the back of the bird, and the pattern will go to where the bird just was.

It's not unusual to miss a clay target with the first shot and hit it with the second. That's because the gun probably never got to the correct position on your cheek for the first shot, but was there—and you focus was right—for the second.

# the stance

The stance is the foundation of good shooting, just as it is in golf or in the batter's box. Trapshooting has been around so long that there are dozens of "correct" stances, some changing with each station. Some skeet shooters like to face the target line directly, others at an angle.

But the following directions, while they can be applied for any form of clays shooting, are basic to sporting clays where targets fly at a larger variety of angles.

Standing with feet placed just inside shoulder-width apart, weight should be evenly distributed and knees flexed. The basic stance for most targets calls for a right-handed shooter to point his or her left toe (right toe for left-handed shooters) toward the point where they intend to break the bird. At address the gun barrel should be held halfway between where the bird is first visible and the breaking point.

This stance will give the shooter the most efficient body position to swing with the flight of the bird.

Again, knees should always be flexed, a factor that is even more critical on dropping targets. As the gun is mounted the weight should be shifted smoothly to the lead foot so that 70 percent of the weight is forward when the trigger is tripped. When done correctly, the left toe and belly button

Shooting instructor Gil Ash explains the effective portion of a shotgun pattern.

should be facing the bird when the shooter fires.

With sufficient practice the shooter will find himself automatically adjusting the stance to address a flushing bird or rabbit in the field.

Although it can't be done in all instances, ideally the gun is fired just as it reaches the shooter's cheek in the practiced position. The Remington Shooting School teaches the "R.E.M Method"—R for read the target, E for eye contact and M for movement. It was actually more like Move, Mount and Shoot but that wouldn't fit the sponsoring company's name as well would it?

# learning the move

A smooth, efficient, practiced move is critical to shooting success, and it starts with pointing the muzzle. One of the basics of Steve Schultz's instruction is the pistol shooting technique—tracking the target with the index finger of your lead hand, not your trigger finger.

He preaches placing the left index finger along the forearm instead of under it, pointing at the target. Holding the gun in this manner allows the shooter the familiar feeling that he's pointing at the target, but it also uses palm and arm (with a locked wrist) as a lever to move the barrel—in much more efficient method than the common palm-under hold.

The one absolutely essential element in successful wingshooting is allowing the lead hand to control the movement, start to finish—sort of like a golf swing. The index finger-point grip of the forend, along with the locked wrist, make the lead arm a very efficient and dependable lever to control the mount and swing of the gun.

It's not only efficient, it's essential. Let the trigger hand take charge at any point, even for a fraction of a second, and the muzzle will move off line.

From a low-gun position, start your move to mount the gun with the lead hand, pointing that index finger toward the target. Let the trigger hand follow but not guide. You do use the trigger hand - to guide the stock up to the ledge of your cheekbone while keeping head still. Put the stock comb there consistently and the butt will automatically slide into position on your shoulder.

It's all got to be one smooth move. Economy of motion. Do what's needed and nothing more. One motion. They say "make haste slowly." Make it deliberate yet fluid.

The typical shooter doesn't do that. He brings the gunbutt up and back

With your lead hand dominating the move, bring the gun smoothly from a low-gun position to a solid cheek weld with your eyes looking directly down the rib.

to his shoulder with trigger hand, drops his head to the stock, then goes looking for the target—which he'll undoubtedly have to chase.

If the trigger hand takes charge the muzzle moves off track. Moving the head short-circuits the essential eye-hand coordination. Go to the shoulder first and the muzzle won't stay on the target path—the lead hand must lead to from start to finish.

Ash and Schultz advise students to practice the mount in front of a mirror, focusing their eyes on the muzzle reflection. Once the correct mount is achieved, it should be repeated on a daily basis to make it an instinctive rather than mechanical move.

A second exercise is to mount the gun and trace the ceiling molding in each direction over and over. Gil Ash preaches inserting a MagLite flashlight into the barrel and using its beam to trace the ceiling lines.

These two exercises repeated in a focused manner 3-4 minutes a day for a couple of weeks will train you surprisingly well.

Experience and practice will permit the shooter to master the combination of physical coordination and mental computation required to become a skilled wingshooter.

# the instinctive shooter

Instinctive shooting is the most commonly taught method, although virtually all instructors (American instructors, anyhow) also teach the sustained lead and pull-through methods to cover all situations.

Instinctive shooting, as Ash teaches it, is coordination between eyes and hands through simple exercises and repetition. Once achieved, that can serve as a foundation for the mastering of specific shooting styles both on clay target ranges and in bird hunting.

Let the mind, the computer, do all the computations when you go after a moving target.

"Sustained lead requires so much computation its almost all experience—there is no consistent way to judge distance against open sky, speed, etc.," said Schultz. "You can compute that a target flying 40 mph at a right angle to you 40 yards away requires 14 feet of lead but what if its actually 35 or 45 yards and coming at an angle of 60 degrees rather than 90?

"Let your brain do the mathematics. It has the capacity if you'll eliminate the obstacles."

Focusing on the target, not the gun's beads or barrel, is the only way for the mind to work correctly.

"You can't see the target when you're looking at the tool," Steve says. Ever try to watch the hammer while you're drying to drive a nail? Do you watch the bat when you're trying to hit a baseball or the club during your golf swing?

If you are looking for shooting instruction—or virtually anything associated with shotgunning—get the latest copy of Black's *Wing & Clay Directory*. The National Shooting Sports Foundation also has a directory of shooting courses at www.wingshooter.com.

## let your mind compensate

"Thinking too much, cluttering the brain with ideas when you actually want it to react instinctively, is a major reason for missing," says master shooting instructor Steve Schultz. "Trust your experience and training. Don't think. It gets in the way.

"Send me the dumb blonde they tell jokes about and I'll have her Olympic caliber in six weeks."

I can testify to the accuracy of Steve's statement. About the shooting, not the dumb blonde.

My original Browning BT-99 trap gun was 25-years-old with a fixed full choke 32-inch barrel when it came to my possession. I shot it several thousand times and was successful with it, but when the opportunity arose to have a screw-in choke system installed, I took it.

The technician at Brileys who did the work asked how the gun patterned. I told him it shot to the requisite height for a trap gun and I'd always assumed that it was dead-on laterally. His gauge instead showed that the barrel patterned four inches right at 20 yards. He straightened it out at my request.

For the first 200 rounds with the new, straight-shooting barrel, I wasn't able to shoot anywhere near my average, and chipped far more targets than normal. The gun simply shot to a different point of aim than I was used to.

I simply kept shooting and the pattern eventually shifted to the point where I was back to shooting my average by the end of a week. The compensation was entirely subconscious. My mind recognized the targets and analyzed the misses, correcting automatically.

Hall of Fame trapshooter Frank Little, who may have been the best there ever was with a shotgun in his hand, always preached that a trapshooter should never pattern his gun. His notion was that knowing the size and character of the gun's pattern would cause the shooter to consciously compensate, which would place his focus somewhere other than where it should be—on the leading edge of that flying target.

Frank was a good friend and hunting buddy but I never got to shoot trap with him before his death in 1994. But I definitely know what he was talking about.

# Shotgun Games

## sporting clays

Sporting clays is a relaxed stroll through a scenic area with stops at target stations situated in the natural habitat, ideally to take advantage of some aspect of the topography.

Each station offers a different look and test of shooting skill. Targets are thrown on command as singles, simultaneous pairs or "report" pairs where the second bird isn't thrown until the first is fired at.

There is no set number of stations and courses vary as much in length as they do in terrain and challenge. It's the closest shooting game to actual hunting—although competition has mitigated that aspect quite a bit in recent years—and has been likened to golf with a shotgun. USA Today in 2004 ranked sporting clays as the second-fastest growing outdoor sport in the nation. It ranked behind snowboarding or some such.

Formal sporting clays competition didn't reach these shores until the 1980s, but the game wasn't a totally foreign concept. Clubs and preserves have had special claybird set-ups for decades, often called "clays" or "crazy quail" courses.

Early in the 20th Century a shooting game was devised in England that incorporated shots from both skeet and trap, plus some other angles. Sporting, as the game was called, was established by some of Britain's top gun makers on their private hunting grounds.

Sporting clays was a derivative of that game and has since become the most popular shooting game in the British Isles. Remington Arms involved the National Rifle Association and the National Shooting Sports Foundation in the introduction of Hunters Clays to North America in the 1960s. Remington-commissioned Briton Chris Craddock to design a course at Remington Farms in Maryland.

The whole idea was to introduce a shooting game that offered far less predictable targets than trap and skeet and one where champions didn't need Mercedes-priced specialty guns and garb and where titles weren't constantly a matter of multi-gun shoot-off among perfect scorers. It was to be a game for which the average upland hunter could use his field gun

*Next page:*
Originally a British invention, sporting clays has become a popular shooting sport with many Americans.

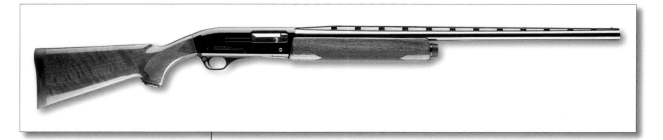

Most target guns feature a raised rib and a parallel comb.

and get useful practice along with a challenge and entertainment.

Remington's introduction proved to be a bit premature as the real interest in sporting clays didn't develop in a major way until world-renowned gun writer Bob Brister of Texas got his first taste of the game on a trip to England in the early 1980s. His coverage of the game persuaded Orvis to involve it in its shooting schools and everything started to snowball.

The first organized sporting clays tournament on record was in 1983 in Brister's Houston. In 1985 the now-defunct United States Sporting Clays Association was formed by a small group of influential Houston shooters and the world heard about it at the Shooting, Hunting and Outdoor Trades (S.H.O.T.) Show in January, 1986.

In 1989 a second organization, the National Sporting Clays Association, was formed as an off-shoot of the National Skeet Shooting Association in San Antonio, Texas. The NSCA is recognized as the sport's sanctioning body in North America today.

# trapshooting

Trapshooting is the oldest of the shotgun games and, until sporting clays grabbed the attention of the masses about 20 years ago, the most popular.

Trap is certainly the most historic and traditional of the games played with a shotgun. It originated in 19th Century England (although there were similar games being shot at least 100 years prior to that), with live pigeons as targets. The pigeons were trapped under top hats and flew when the hats were tipped by a string operated by the "puller."

As the game grew, box traps replaced the top hats and glass balls filled with feathers or soot replaced the pigeons. Eventually brightly colored, easy-to-throw clay disks became the targets.

Today competitors shoot rounds of 25 birds, five from each of five positions arrayed equidistantly behind the traphouse, a bunker that houses a rotating trap, or bird-throwing device.

The targets are thrown, on command, in random directions dictated by the constantly moving trap head, always flying away from the shooter. Trapshooters use moderate to tightly choked 12-gauge guns with raised barrel ribs to make them shoot high, since the targets are rising. All of the targets are going away from the shooter at a longer distance and tighter angle than most skeet or sporting clays targets.

Singles trap, which is the basic form of the game, is contested with all competitors shooting from the 16-yard line behind the traphouse. In handicap trap everything is the same except that the shooter is moved back, being placed according to experience and ability, to a limit of 27 yards from the traphouse. In doubles the shooter again toes the 16-yard line at each of five stations where he shoots simultaneous pairs thrown at predetermined angles.

Visually, trapshooting would seem to be the easiest of the shotgun games. But the random path of the targets, combined with the distance of the shots (shooters ideally break targets at 32 yards in singles, up to 45 inch handicap) and the variety of angles make it difficult. For talented shooters one of the biggest obstacles to overcome is maintaining focus while wading through 100 shots in a match.

There is an international version of trap, which is contested at the Olympics. There the targets are thrown faster, from a wider variety of angles, from multiple traps.

Singles trap is contested from five stations each located 16 yards behind the trap house.

The American version of the game held its world championships, the Grand American Championships, at Vandalia, Ohio, for more than 80 years prior to its move to Sparta, Illinois, in 2006.

At Vandalia the "Grand" had been held on a mile-long line of traps on the outskirts of the Dayton International Airport, giving the competitors a unique backdrop of taxiing airplanes, opening and closing hangar doors and the control tower.

But progress and commerce overcame tradition and the airport's expansion plans simply crowded out 100-plus year-old event. The new World Shooting Complex in Sparta, outside of St. Louis, now hosts the Grand American as its anchor event.

# what is skeet shooting?

Skeet evolved from trapshooting in the 1920s when New Englander Charles Davies, dissatisfied with trap's lack of crossover and incoming shots, set out to develop a game that offered more shots encountered while hunting.

An American skeet field today has eight shooting positions, seven of which are arranged in a half-circle facing the line between the two tall traphouses. The eighth is directly between the traps. The left-hand house is elevated much higher than the right.

At each station contestants shoot one target from each house. On stations No. 1, 2, 6 and 7 they also shoot doubles, targets released simultaneously from the two houses. Twenty-five targets is considered a round. Unlike trapshooting, which is essentially a 12-gauge game, skeet is contested in 12-, 20-, 28- and .410-gauge and doubles.

There is also an international version which features longer shots at faster targets. Contestants must carry the gun from a "low" position and

Skeet shooter with high house in background.

mount it while the bird is flying, rather than standing with a mounted gun as in the American game.

Skeet's hard crossing angles make its targets seem more difficult than trap. But in actuality it's a mechanical game since the target angles and paths—all short range (22 yards)—are known prior to the shot and executing is simply a matter of knowing (and practicing) the proper lead and swing speed.

It's a little known fact that complaints from a neighbor in 1926 changed skeet shooting to the format that is followed today.

Davies, of Andover, Massachusetts, is credited with devising the original game of "Shooting Around the Clock" in which one trap was used and shooters moved around it in a circle. When a neighbor complained about direction of the shooting, Davies cut the circle in half and added a second trap opposite the first, which he eventually raised to add variety.

The National Sportsman magazine promoted the game but by 1926 it lacked a good name and the magazine ran a contest to get it a name. The $100 first prize went to a woman who submitted the name 'skeet' which is a Scandanavian term for 'shoot.'

# games for hunting practice

Two or three generations ago chances were the hunter in the family was a pretty fair wingshot. Guns and loads were nowhere as effective or efficient as they are today, but back then a man could learn to shoot in the field. Bag limits were generous or unheard-of and game was plentiful. If he missed or made a mistake—prime elements of the learning process —there was always another opportunity.

But hunting today is different. Small bag limits, limited venues, time constraints, more hunter competition on less ground and a general lack of game makes it virtually impossible for the average gunner to improve, let alone perfect his shotgunning technique, in true hunting situations.

If your principal interest, like mine, lies in the hedgerows, culverts, marshes and fields you have an obligation to yourself and to the birds and small game to become a better field shot.

Lucky for hunters there alternatives to field experience called shooting games—trap, skeet and sporting clays. Right?

Well, trap and skeet were originated to provide practice for bird hunters but over the years the two games have evolved into rigid, fixed target events for shooters with mounted guns on courses that are identical from locale to locale. Where's the field practice there?

The game of sporting clays also emerged as practice drill for field shooting. But even that game has become, well, a game. The serious sporting clays shooter today wants a 30-34-inch barrel for better swing; changes chokes station-to-station based on the distance of the shot; asks to see the target before going to the shooting position. Hell, they even shoot the game with a mounted gun now.

Nothing wrong with that. That's simply how the games are played

now. They are competitive, enjoyable, challenging games unto themselves, not field practice.

But that doesn't mean that their respective courses can't still be used for real field shooting practice.

Try these drills, starting with your hunting gun held low as it would be in the field:

### trap field:

Pick any station and, from the 27-yard-line, start walking, head-down toward the traphouse. Have a buddy throw a target without your knowing when or where, then sight the target and move to break it. Also try this drill while walking laterally across the field, perpendicular to the target line. Try 20-30 of these, from as many different positions and you'll have a productive and meaningful round of field-shooting practice.

### skeet field:

This one is good practice for quick, in-the-woods grouse shots. Again pick any position on the field and stand at any angle to the target line, and have a buddy throw a bird from either house at his discretion. You should restrict your hearing in this drill, so that you won't recognize which trap has been tripped, instead having your buddy yell "bird!" as he would in the field. Reacting to his command, sight the target quickly and move to break it. Twenty or 30 of these will be humbling but the more you do it, the more natural and fluid the quick, angled move will become.

### sporting clays course:

Approach each station without knowing the targets or angles and stand as you would in the field—off to the side of the stand if possible—while someone pulls a target on their own timing. Again, your hearing should be muffled here so that you don't recognize the direction of the trap by its sound. React to your buddy's command, locate the bird and move to break it. This one is real practice and can actually be used as your "sighter" while shooting a practice round of sporting clays.

# appendix - products

## SHOTGUNS

**Benelli-Stoeger-Franchi**
17603 Indian Head Hwy
Accokeek, MD 20607
301-283-6981
www.benelliusa.com
www.franchiusa.com

**Beretta USA**
17601 Beretta Drive
Accokeek, MD 20607
301-283-2191
www.berettausa.com

**Thomas Bland & Sons**
Woodcock Hill Inc.
192 Spencers Rd.
PO Box 363
Benton, PA 17814
570-864-3242
www.woodcockhill.com

**Browning**
One Browning Place
Morgan, UT 84050
(801) 876-2711
www.browning.com

**BSA Imports**
3911 SW 47th Ave., Suite 914
Ft. Lauderdale, FL
(954) 581-2047

**Charles Daly**
K.B.I. Inc.
P.O. Box 6625
Harrisburg, PA 17112
866-DALYGUN
www.charlesdaly.com

**Connecticut Shotgun Company**
35 Woodland Street
New Britain, CT 06501
860-225-6681
www.connecticutshotgun.com

**Dakota Arms**
1310 Industry Road
Sturgis, SD 57785
605-347-4686
www.dakotaarms.com

**European American Armory**
PO Box 1299
Sharpes, FL 32959
321-639-4842
www.eaacorp.com

**Griffin & Howe**
36 West 44th St., Suite 1011
New York, NY 10036
212-921-0980
www.griffinhowe.com

**Heckler & Koch, Inc.**
(Fabarms)
21480 Pacific Blvd.
Sterling, VA 22170-8903
703-450-1900
www.hecklerkoch-usa.com

**Holland & Holland**
50 East 57th St.
New York, NY 10022
212-752-7755
www.hollandholland.com

**Ithaca Guns USA**
420 N. Warpole Street
Upper Sandusk, OH 43351
www.ithacagunsUSA.com

**Krieghoff International**
PO Box 549
Ottsville, PA 18942
610-847-5173
www.krieghoff.com

**Legacy Sports International**
(Escort, Silma, Kahn)
206 South Union Street
Alexandria, VA 22314
(703) 548-4837
www.legacysports.com

**Ljutic Industries**
732 N. 16th Ave.
Yakima, WA 98902
509-248-0476

**Marlin Firearms Co.**
100 Kenna Drive
North Haven, CT 06473
203-239-5621
www.marlinfirearms.com

**Merkel**
% GSI Inc.
7661 Commerce Lane
Trussville, AL 35173
205-655-8299
www.gsifirearms.com

**New England Firearms Co., Inc.**
(also H&R 1871)
Industrial Rowe
Gardner, MA 01440
978-632-9393

**O.F. Mossberg & Sons, Inc.**
7 Grasso Avenue
North Haven, CT 06473
203-230-5300
www.mossberg.com

**Parker Bros. Makers**
Meriden, Conn.
203-206-7287
www.parkerbrosmakers.com

**Parker Reproduction Shotguns**
114 Broad Street
Flemington, NJ 08822
908-284-2800

**Perazzi USA inc.**
855 North Todd Ave.
Azusa, CA 91741
626-334-1234
perazziusa@aol.com

**James Purdey & Sons**
57-58 South Audley St.
London
W1K 2ED United Kingdom
Enquries@james-purdey.co.uk

**Remington Arms Co., Inc.**
870 Remington Drive
P.O. Box 700
Madison, NC 27025-0700
800-243-9700
www.remington.com

**Renato Gamba (Carrera)**
21027 NE Hwy 27
Williston, FL 32696
800-226-3613
rhinoman@atlantic.net

**Rizinni SRI**
Via 2 Giugno
7/7bis Marcheno
Brescia, Italy 25060
www.rizzini.com

**SKB Shotguns**
4325 South 120th Street
Omaha, NE 68137
800-752-2767
www.skbshotguns.com

**Sturm, Ruger & Co.**
200 Ruger Road
Prescott, AZ 86301
520-541-8820
www.ruger-firearms.com

**Tar-Hunt Slug Guns**
101 Dogtown Road
Bloomsburg, PA 17815
570-784-6368
www.tar-hunt.com

**Traditions Performance Firearms**
1375 Boston Post Road
Old Saybrook, CT 06475
860-388-4656
www.traditionsfirearms.com

**U.S. Repeating Arms**
(Winchester Firearms)
275 Winchester Avenue
Morgan, UT 84050-9333
801-876-3440
www.winchester-guns.com

**Weatherby, Inc.**
3100 El Camino Real
Atascadero, CA 93422
800-227-2016
www.weatherby.com

## MUZZLELOADING SHOTGUNS

**Blackpowder Products, Inc.**
(Winchester-CVA)
5988 Peachtree Corners East
Norcross, GA 30071
(877)892-7544
www.winchestermuzzleloading.com
www.cva.com
www.bpiguns.com

**Modern Muzzleloading**
(Knight Rifles)
(866) 518-4181
www.knightrifles.com

**Savage Arms**
100 Springdale Road
Westfield, MA 01085
(413) 568-7001
www.SavageArms.com

**Thompson Center Arms**
PO Box 5002
Rochester, NH 03866
(603) 332-2394
www.tcarms.com

## AMMUNITION

**Aguila**
Centurion Ordnance
11614 Rainbow Ridge
Helotes, TX 78023
(210) 695-4602
www.aguilaammo.com

**All-Purpose Ammo**
515 Concord Ind. Drive
Seneca, SC 29672
800-870-2666

**Brenneke of America**
P.O. Box 1481
Clinton, IA 52733
800-753-9733
www.brennekeusa.com

**Bismuth Cartridge Co.**
11650 Riverside Drove
N. Hollywood, CA 91602
800-759-3333
www.bismuth-notox.com

**Dynamit-Nobel/RWS**
81 Ruckman Road
Closter, NJ 07624
201-767-1995
www.dnrws.com

**Estate Cartridge**
900 Ehlen Drive
Anoka, MN 55303
800-322-2342
www.estatecartridge.com

**Federal Cartridge Company**
900 Ehlen Drive
Anoka, MN 55303
763-323-3834
www.federalcartridge.com

**Fiocchi of America**
6930 Fremont Road
Ozark, MO 65721
417-725-4118
www.fiocchiusa.com

**Hevi-Shot**
EnvironMetal, Inc.
1307 Clark Mill Road
Sweet Home, OR 97386
541-367-3522
Hevishot@aol.com

**Hornady Manufacturing**
3625 Old Potash Highway
Grand Island, NE 68803
308-382-1390
www.hornady.com

**Kent Cartridge**
10000 Zigor Road
Kearneysville, WV 25430
888-311-KENT
www.kentgamebore.com

**Lightfield Ammunition**
P.O. Box 162
Adelphia, NJ 07710
732-462-9200
www.lightfield-ammo.com

**Nitro Company Ammunition**
7560 Newkirk Rd.
Mountain Grove, MO 65711
417-746-4600
www.nitrocompany.com

**Orion Cartridge Co.**
Box 1258
Camden, SC 29020
800-642-4110
orion@camden.net

**PMC Ammunition**
P.O. Box 62508
Boulder City, NV 89006
702-294-0025
www.pmcammo.com

**Polywad Shotgun Shells**
P.O. Box 7916
Macon, GA 31209
800-998-0669
www.polywad.com

**Remington, Inc.**
870 Remington Drive
P.O. Box 700
Madison, NC 27025-0700
800-243-9700
www.remington.com

**Rio Ammunition**
5892 Hwy 230 West
McEwen, TN 37101
www.rioammo.com

**Royal Sporting Ltd.**
1633 Mount Vernon Road
Dunwoody, GA 30338
800-404-1000
www.royalsportingltd.com

**RST Ltd.**
7 Weston Way
Center Conway, NH 03813
603-447-6769

**Sellier & Bellot, USA**
P.O. Box 7307
Shawnee Mission, KS 66207
800-960-2422
ceg@sb-usa.com

**Winchester/Olin**
427 N. Shamrock Street
East Alton, IL 62024-1174
618-258-2204
www.winchester.com

**Wolf Performance Ammunition**
2201 E. Winston Road, Suite K
Anaheim, CA 92806
888-757-WOLF
www.wolfammo.com

## CHOKE TUBES AND TUBESETS

**Angle Porting**
By Ballistic Specialties
P.O. Box 2401
Batesville, AR 72503
800-276-2550
www.angleport.com

**Stan Baker Barrels**
10000 Lake City Way
Seattle, WA 98125
206-522-4575

**Bansner's Custom Gunsmithing**
261 East Main Street
Adamstown, PA 19501
717-484-2370

**Briley Manufacturing**
1230 Lumpkin
Houston, TX 77043
800-331-5718
www.briley.com

**Carlson's**
P.O. Box 162
Atwood, KS 67730
785-626-3700

**Cation**
(Sniper choke tubes)
2341 Alger Street
Troy, MI 48083
810-689-0658
cation@mich.com

**Clear View Products**
3021 N. Portland
Oklahoma City, OK 73107
405-943-9222

**Colonial Arms**
1109C Singleton Dr.

Selma, AL 36702
800-949-8088
www.colonialarms.com
**Comp-N-Choke**
925 Waynesboro Highway
Sylvania, GA 30467
888-875-7906
www.comp-n-choke.com
**Hastings Barrels**
Kebco LLC
P.O. Box 300
Hanover, PA 17331
(717) 524-5301
www.hastingsbarrels.com
**Haydel's Game Calls**
5018 Hazel Jones Road
Bossier City, LA 71111
800-HAYDELS
www.haydels.com
**Highlander Sports**
3004 11th Avenue SW
Huntsville, AL 35805
800-758-2346
curtis@highlandersports.com
**Kick's Industries**
925 Waynesboro Highway
Sylvania, GA 30467
888-587-2779
www.kicks-ind.com
**Lohman Marsh Max**
Outland Sports
4500 Doniphan Drive
Neosho, MO 64850
900-922-9034
**Marble Arms/Poly-Choke**
P.O. Box 111
Gladstone, MI 49837
906-428-3710
**Nu-Line Guns**
1053 Caulks Hill Road
Harvester, MO 63304
636-441-4500
nulineguns@nulineguns.com
**Patternmaster**
6431 North Taos Road
Scott City, KS 67871
620-872-3022
**Pure Gold Premium**
2211 Ogden Road
Rock Hill, SC 29730
803-328-6829
gameacc@cetlimk.net
**Rhino Chokes**
21890 NE Highway 27
Williston, FL 32696
800-226-3613
rhinoman@atlantic.net
**Seminole Gunworks**
3049 US Route 1
Mims, FL 32754
800-980-3344
www.seminolegun.com
**Truglo**
13745 Neutron Drive
Dallas, TX 75244
972-774-0300
www.truglosights.com
**Trulock Chokes**
102 E. Broad Street
Whigham, GA 31797
800-293-9402
www.trulockchokes.com
**Wright's, Inc.**
4591 Shotgun Alley
Pinckneyville, IL 62274
618-357-8933
www.wrightschokes.com

## GUN CARE PRODUCTS
**Beretta Gallery**
718 Madison Ave.
New York, NY 10021
212-319-3235
www.berettausa.com
**Birchwood Casey**
7900 Fuller Rd.
Eden Prairie, MN 55344
800-328-6156
www.birchwoodcasey.com
**BoreSnake**
GunMate

PO Box 1720
Oregon City, OR 97045
503-655-2837
**Bore Tech Inc.**
2950 N. Advance Lane
Colmar, PA 18915
215-997-9689
www.boretech.com
**Break-Free Inc.**
An Armor Holdings
13386 International Pkwy
Jacksonville, FL 32218
800-428-0588
www.break-free.com
**Chem-Pak Inc.**
242 Corning Way
Martinsburg, WV 25401
800-336-9828
www.chem-pak.com
**Choke Shine**
G.E.M.S. Inc.
33717 Hwy 23
Collins, GA 30421
888-507-8762
www.chokeshine.com
**Corrosion Technologies**
PO Box 551625
Dallas, TX 75355-1625
800-638-7361
corrosnx@ix.netcom.com
**J. Dewey Rods**
PO Box 2104
Southbury, CT 06488
203-264-3064
**DSX Products**
M.S.R. Inc.
PO Box 1372
Sterling, VA 20167-1372
800-822-0258
**Du-Lite Corp.**
171 River Rd.
Middletown, CT 06457
860-347-2505
**EEZOX Inc.**
PO Box 772
Waterford, CT 06385
800-462-3331
**Flitz International**
821 Mohr Ave.
Waterford, WI 53185
800-558-8611
www.flitz.com
**Free Gun Cleaner**
Frigon Guns
1605 Broughton Rd.
Clay Center, KS 67432
785-632-5607
**Golden Bore Gun Care**
Termark International
200 W. 17th St.
Cheyenne, WY 82001
888-483-7677
goldenbore@usa.net
**Gunslick**
PO Box 39
Onalaska, WI 54650
800-635-7656
**H&R Outdoors**
914 Artic St.
Bridgeport, CT 06608
888-761-4250
**Hoppes**
Div. of Michaels of Oregon
Airport Industrial Mall
Coatesville, PA 19320
610-384-6000
www.hoppes.com
**The Inhibitor**
Van Patten Industries
PO Box 6694
Rockford, IL 61125
815-332-4812
www.theinhibitor.com
**International Lubrication Labs**
1895 East 56 Rd.
Lecompton, KS 66050
785-887-6004
**Iosso Products**
1485 Lively Blvd.
Elk Grove, IL 60007
847-437-8400

www.iosso.com
**Kleen-Bore Inc.**
16 Industrial Pkwy
Easthampton, MA 01027
800-445-0301
**Mpro7 Gun Care**
Windfall Inc.
PO Box 54988
225 W. Deer Valley Rd. #4
Phoenix, AZ 85078
800-YES-4MP7
**Ms Moly Ballistic Conditioner**
1952 Knob Rd.
Burlington, WI 53105
800-264-4140
**MTM Molded Products**
3370 Obco Court
Dayton, OH 45413
513-890-7461
**Neco**
536 C. Stone Rd.
Benicia, CA 94510
707-747-0897
**Otis Technology**
PO Box 582
Lyons Falls, NY 13368
800-OTISGUN
www.otisgun.com
**Outers**
PO Box 38
Onalaska, WI 54650
608-781-5800
**Ox-Yoke Originals**
34 West Main St.
Milo, ME 04463
207-943-7351
**Peak Enterprises**
79 Bailey Dr.
Newman, GA 30263
770-253-1397
tpeak@west.ga.net
**Prolix**
div. Pro-ChemCo
PO Box 1348
Victorville, CA 92393-1348
760-243-3129
prolix@accex.net
**Pro-Shot Products**
PO Box 763
Taylorsville, IL 62568
217-824-9133
www.proshotproducts.com
**ProTec International**
1747 Bartlett Rd.
Memphis, TN 38134
800-843-5649 ext. 101
sales@proteclubricants.com
**Rapid Rod**
ATSKO Inc.
2664 Russell St.
Orangeburg, SC 29115
800-845-2728
info@atsko.com
**Rig Products**
56 Coney Island Dr.
Sparks, NV 89509
775-359-4451
**Rusteprufe Labs**
1319 Jefferson Ave.
Sparta, WI 54656
608-269-4144
rusteprufe@centurytel.net
**Salvo Industries**
5173 N. Douglas Fir Rd.
Calabasas, CA 91302
818-222-2276
jacob@ammotech.com
**Sentry Solutions**
111 Sugar Hill Rd.
Contoocook, NH 03229
603-746-5687
bwc@sentrysolutions.com
**Shooters Choice Gun Care**
c/o Ventco Industries
15050 Berkshire Industrial Pkwy
Middlefield, OH 44062
440-834-8888
shooters@shooter-choice.com
**Sinclair International**
2330 Wayne Haven St.
Fort Wayne, IN 46803

260-493-1858
www.sinclairintl.com
**Slip 2000**
Superior Products
355 Mandela Pkwy
Oakland, CA 94607
707-585-8329
www.slip2000.com
**Sports Care Products**
PO Box 589
Aurora, OH 44202
888-428-8840
**TDP Industries**
606 Airport Rd.
Doylestown, PA 18901
215-345-8687
**Tetra Gun Care**
FTI Inc.
8 Vreeland Rd.
Florham Park, NJ 07932
973-443-0004
**Thunder Products**
PO Box H
San Jose, CA 95151
408-270-4200
**Tipton**
c/o Battenfeld Technologies
5885 W. VanHorn Tavern Rd.
Columbia, MO 65203
877-509-9160
www.battenfeldtechnologies.com
**White Lightning**
Leisure Innovations
1545 Fifth Industrial Ct.
Bay Shore, NY 11706
800-390-9222

## RELOADING EQUIPMENT
**Battenfeld Technologies**
5875 West Van Horn Tavern Road
Columbia, MO 65203
877-509-9160
www.battenfeldtechnologies.com
**Brownells, Inc.**
200 South Front St.
Montezuma, IA 50171
641-623-5401
www.brownells.com
**Dillon Precision**
8009 E. Dillon's Way
Scottsdale, AZ 85260
602-948-8009
www.dillonprecision.com
**Hornady Mfg.**
Box 1848
Grand Island, NE 68802
308-382-1390
**Lee Precision**
4275 Highway U
Hartford, WI 53027
262-673-3075
**MEC**
Mayfield Engineering
715 South St.
Mayville, WI 53050
920-387-4500
www.mecreloaders.com
**Midway USA**
5875 West Van Horn Tavern Road
Columbia, MO 65203
573-445-6363
www.midwayusa.com
**Ponsness/Warren**
768 Ohio St.
Rathdrum, ID 83858
208-687-2231
bsteele@reloaders.com
**RCBS**
PO Box 39
Onalaska, WI 54650
800-635-7656
www.outers-guncare.com
**Spolar Power Load**
2273 S. Vista B-2
Bloomington, CA 92316
800-227-9667
www.spolargold.com

## POWDERS-RELOADING COMPONENTS
**Accurate Arms**

5891 Highway 230 West
McEwen, TN 37101
800-416-3006
www.accuratepowder.com

**ADCO/NobelSport**
4 Draper St.
Woburn, MA 01801
781-935-1799
www.adcosales.com

**Alaskan Cartridge**
RR2 Box 192F
Hastings, NE 68901-9408
402-463-3415

**Alliant Powder Co.**
PO Box 4
State Rte. 114
Radford, VA 21141-0096
800-276-9337
dick-quesenberry@atk.com

**Ball Powder Propellant**
St. Marks Powder
PO Box 222
St. Marks, FL 32355
850-577-2273
srfaintich@stm.gd-ots.com

**Ballistic Products, Inc.**
P.O. Box 293
Hamel, MN 55340
763-494-9237
www.ballisticproducts.com

**Claybuster Wads**
C&D Special Products
309 Sequoya Dr.
Hopkinsville, Ky 42240
502-885-8088
dmac@spis.net

**Clean Shot Technologies**
21218 St. Andrews Blvd #504
Boca Raton, FL 33433
888-419-2073
cleanshot@aol.com

**Duster Wads**
Micro Technologies
1405 Laukant St.
Reedsburg, WI 53959
888-438-7837

**Hodgdon Powder**
6231 Robinson
Shawnee Mission, KS 66201
913-362-9455
info@hodgdon.com

**IMR Powder**
6733 Mississauga Rd., Suite 306
Mississauga, Ontario
Canada L5N 6J5
520-393-1600
www.imrpowder.com

**Lawrence Brand Shot**
Metalico-Granite City
1200 16th St.
Granite City, IL 62040
618-451-4400

**Polywad Spred-R**
PO Box 7916
Macon, GA 31209
800-998-0669
www.polywad.com

**Reloading Specialties**
52901 265th Ave.
Pine Island, MN 55963
507-356-8500

**Sabot Technologies**
P.O. Box 189
Alum Bank, PA 15521-0189
877-704-4868
www.sabottechnologies.com
www.slugsRus.com

**Vihtavuori/Lapua**
Kalton-Pettibone
1241 Ellis St.
Bensenville, IL 60106
800-683-0464
jbolda@kaltron.com

**RamShot Powders**
c/oWestern Powders
PO Box 158
Yellowstone Hill
Miles City, MT 59301
800-497-1007
powder@midrivers.com

## SHOOTING SCHOOLS

**AAClaybusters LLC**
Seattle, WA
877-783-4576
aaclaybusters@att.net

**Addieville East Farm**
Maplesville, RI
401-568-3185
www.addieville.com

**Arnold's Custom Shooting Sports**
Camden, OH
937-787-3352
www.customshooting.com

**LL Bean Shooting School**
Freeport, ME
888-552-3261

**Bender Shima Shooting Clinics**
Alpharetta, GA
678-296-5184
bender285@aol.com

**Big Moore's Run Lodge**
Coudersport, PA
866-569-3474

**Blackwater Training Co.**
Moyock, NC
252-435-2488
billm@blackwaterlodge.com

**Pete Blakeley Shooting School**
Lewisville, TX
972-462-0043
www.dallasgunclub.com

**British School of Shooting**
St. Simons Island, GA
912-656-1587
jonestheshoot@aol.com

**Broxton Bridge Plantation**
Ehrhardt, SC
800-437-4868

**Carlisle's Shooting School**
Phenix City, AL
334-297-1910

**Deep River Shooting School**
Sanford, NC
919-774-7080
www.deepriver.net

**Andy Duffy Clinics**
Wakefield, RI
401-741-5076

**Elite Shooting School**
Houston, TX
713-334-0656
elitegun@aol.com

**Buz Fawcett's Wingshooting**
Meridian, ID
208-888-3415

**FieldSport**
Traverse City, MI
231-933-0767
www.fieldsportltd.com

**Connie Fournier/ISA**
Bethel Park, PA
412-835-5749
gunteach@bellatlantic.net

**Friar Tuck Wing & Clay School**
Catskill, NY
800-832-7600 ext447
www.friartucksingandclay.com

**Les Greevy's West Branch
Shooting School**
Williamsport, PA
570-326-6561
greevy@mail.microserve.net

**Griffin & Howe Shooting Schools**
Bernardsville, NJ
908-766-2287
www.griffinhowe.com

**Gun Room at Robin Hollow**
Wickford, RI
401-267-0102
www.robinhollow.com

**Gun Site Academy**
Paulden, AZ
520-636-4565

**Jo Hanley Shooting Instruction**
West Palm Beach, FL
561-881-8323
joshot@excelonline.com

**Holland & Holland Sporting**
New York, NY
212-752-7755
www.hollandandholland.com

**The Homestead Shooting School**
Hot Springs, VA
540-839-7787

**Mick Howell's Shooting School**
Wellington, IL
561-792-0038
mickhowel@aol.com

**Hunter's Creek Club**
Metamora, MI
810-664-4307
www.hunterscreekclub.com

**Instinctive Target Interception**
Shotgun Shooting School
Albuquerque, NM
505-836-1206
itishooting@juno.com

**Instructional Shooting**
Lowell, MA
978-452-8450
www.agguns.com

**J&P Shooting School**
Sudlersville, MD
410-438-3832
staff@jphuntinglodge.com

**Jamison Shotgun Sports**
Denver, CO
303-745-3840

**Joshua Creek Ranch**
Boerne, TX
830-537-5090
www.joshuacreek.com

**Phil Kiner Trapshooting Clinics**
Cheyenne, WY
307-635-1451

**John Kruger Shooting Enterprises**
Sunman, IN
812-926-4999
www.quailridgeclub.com

**Longshot Shooting School**
Broken Arrow, OK
800-348-1111

**Keith Lupton Shooting Schools**
Dover Plains, NY
845-877-3719

**Middleditch Shooting School**
Orlando, FL
407-380-9533

**Midwest Shooting School**
Wrenshall, MN
218-384-3670
www.midwestshootingschool.com

**Dan Mitchell's Clay and
Wingshooting School**
Brooks, OR
503-792-3431
danidaho@insn.com

**Mt. Blanca Lodge**
Blanca, CO
800-686-4024

**Michael Murphy & Sons**
Augusta, KS
316-775-2137
www.murphyshotguns.com

**National Wing & Clay School**
Woodland, WA
360-225-5000
info@shootinginstruction.com

**Kay Ohye Trap School**
North Brunswick, NJ
732-297-0364

**On Target**
Yorba Linda, CA
714-970-8072
jbraccini@aol.com

**Optimum Shotgun Performance
Shooting School**
(Gil and Vicki Ash)
Houston, TX
800-838-7533
www.ospschool.com

**Orvis Shooting Schools**
Manchester, VT
800-235-9763
www.orvis.com

**Outdoors Unlimited
Shooting School**
Eagle Lake, TX
979-234-5750

**Paint Creek Shooting School**
Metamora, MI
248-814-9191 Ex19

faermark@hotmail.com

**Paradise Outfitters**
Small Gauge Academy
Bellwood, PA
814-742-3297

**Paragon School of Sporting**
Flat Rock, NC
828-693-6600
www.paragonschool.com

**Peace Dale Shooting School**
Peace Dale, RI
401-789-3730
pdshootrichf@aol.com

**Gary Phillips Shooting Instruction**
Wilmington, DE
302-655-7113
gphilgun1@aol.com

**Pintail Point Shooting School**
Queenstown, MD
410-827-7029
www.pintailpoint.com

**Prairie Moon Ranch**
San Antonio, TX
210-732-8765
www.clayschool.com

**Recreational Shooting
Sports Service**
San Antonio, TX
210-543-7014
dgmose74@gateway.net

**Rock Run Sports Club**
Coatesville, PA
610-383-1000
www.rockrunclub.com

**Scattergun Wingshooting School**
Seffner, FL
813-684-6211
fwilson@tampabay.rr.com

**Sea Island Shooting School**
Sea Island, GA
800-SEA-ISLAND
bobedwards@seaisland.com

**Shoot Where You Look**
Livingston, TX
800-201-5535

**Shooting Academy at Nemacolin
Woodlands**
Farmington, PA
800-422-2736
clays@nwlr.com
www.nemacolin.com

**Shooting Sports Unlimited**
Lanai City, HI
808-563-1533
clays@aloha.net

**TM Ranch Shotgun Sports**
Orlando, FL
407-737-3788
tmranch@bellsouth.net

**Taddlinger's Shooting School**
Wilmington, VT
802-464-1223

**Target Line Shooting School**
McAllen, TX
956-682-1260
sschultz52@aol.com

**Texas Academy of Wingshooting**
Friendswood, TX
713-725-9876

**Texas Wingshooting Sports**
Whitewright, TX
903-364-2076
texaspa2@gte.net

**Thunder Ranch**
Mountain Home, TX
830-640-3138

**Top Gun Shooting Schools**
Kewaskum, WI
262-626-6640
dftopgun@nconnect.net

**Angelo Troisi Skeet Shooting Clinic**
Andover, MA
978-470-3481
shinespapa@mediaone.net

**Victory Shooting School**
Columbia, MO
573-442-9189
mbsportpsych@netscape.net

**The Willow**
Robinsville, MS
662-357-3154

danielsb@grandcasinos.com
**Wings & Clays Shooting School**
Lake Orion, MI
800-SHO-TGUN
**Wise Wingshooting Academy**
Chestertown, MD
410-778-4950
benwise@friend.ly.net
**Woodcock Hill**
Benton, PA
570-864-3242
bland@epix.net

## ORGANIZATIONS
**Amateur Trapshooting Association**
601 W. National Road
Vandalia, OH 45377
932-898-4638
www.shootata.com
**National Reloading Manufacturers Association**
One Centerpoint Drive 300
Lake Oswego, OR 97035
**National Rifle Association**
11250 Waples Mill Road
Fairfax, VA 22030
703-267-1000
www.nra.org
**National Shooting Sports Foundation**
11 Mile Hill Rd.
Flintlock Ridge Office Center
Newton, CT 06470
203-426-1320
www.nssf.com
**National Skeet Shooting Association**
5931 Roft Road
San Antonio, TX 78253
210-688-3371
**National Sporting Clays Association**
5931 Roft Road
San Antonio, TX 78253
210-688-3371
**North American Side-by-Side Association**
137 Shrewsbury Street
West Boylston, MA 01583
508-835-6057
ewfosterjr.@aol.com
**PRO/AM Shotgun Society**
P.O. Box 3
Mims, FL 32754
904-345-0485
pass@sportingclays.com
**Scholastic Clay Target Program**
P.O. Box 872
Blacksburg, VA 24063
540-951-1569
wrchristy@mindspring.com
**Sporting Arms & Ammunition Manufacturers Institute**
11 Mile Hill Road
Flintlock Ridge Office Center
Newton, CT 06470
203-426-1320
www.nssf.com
**Sporting Clays of America**
9257 Buckeye Road
Sugar Grove, OH 43155
740-746-8334
**World Sporting Clays Network**
2625 Piedmont Road NE
Atlanta, GA 30324
404-266-0202
wcsn@aol.com

## OTHER CONTACTS
**American Gunsmithing Institute**
1325 Imola Avenue, W. 504
Napa, CA 94559
707-253-0462
www.americangunsmith.com
**Black's Wing & Clay Directory**
PO Box 2029
Red Bank, NJ 07701
732-224-8700
blacksporting@msn.com
**Second Skin Camo**
3434 Buck Mt. Road
Roanoke, VA 24014

540-774-9248
www.trebark.com
**300 Below Cryogenic Tempering**
2999 Parkway Drive
Decatur, IL 62526
217-423-3070
www.300below.com

## OPTICS
**ADCO Sales**
4 Draper St.
Woburn, MA 01801
www.adcosales.com
**Aimpoint**
7702 Leesburg Pike
Falls Church, VA 22043
877-246-7646
www.aimpoint.com
**AO Sight Systems**
XS Sight Systems
2401 Ludelle St.
Fort Worth, TX 76105
888-744-4880
www.xssights.com
**BSA Sport**
3911 SW 47th Av  Suite 914
Ft. Lauderdale, FL 33314
945-581-2144
www.bsaoptics.com
**Burris Company**
331 East 8th St.
Greeley, CO 80631-9559
970-356-1670
www.burrisoptics.com
**Bushnell Performance Optics**
(also Tasco)
9200 Cody
Overland Park, KS 66214
800-423-3537
www.bushnell.com
www.tasco.com
**Deutsche Optik**
P.O. Box 601114
San Diego, CA 92160-1114
800-225-9407
www.deutscheoptik.com
**Fujinon Inc.**
10 High Point Dr.
Wayne, NJ 07470
973-633-5600
www.fujinon.jp.com
**HiViz Shooting Systems**
1841 Heath Pkway.  Suite 1
Fort Collins, CO 80524
800-589-4315
www.hivizsights.com
**Hunter Wicked Optics**
3300 W.71st Ave.
Westminster, CO 80030-5303
800-676-4868
www.huntercompany.com
**Ironsighter Company**
P.O. Box 85070
Westland, MI 48185
734-326-8731
www.ironsighter.com
**Leatherwood/Hi-Lux Optics**
2535 West 237th St. Suite 106
Torrance, CA 90505
310-257-8142
www.leatherwoodoptics.com
**Legacy Sports Internat l**
(Nikko-Stirling Scopes)
206 South Union St.
Alexandria, VA 22314
703-548-4837
www.legacysports.com
**Leupold & Stevens**
14400 NW Greenbriar Pkwy.
Beaverton, OR 97006
503-646-9171
www.leupold.com
**Millett Sights**
16131-K Gothard St.
Huntington Beach, CA 92647
714-842-5575
www.millettsights.com
**Nikon Sports Optics**
1300 Walt Whitman Rd.
Melville, NY 11747
631-547-4200

www.nikonusa.com
**Pentax USA**
35Inverness Dr. East
Englewood, CO 80112
800-877-1255
www.pentaxlightseeker.com
**Redfield USA**
Redfield Scopes
P.O. Box 688
14400 NW Greenbrier Parkway
Beaverton, OR 97006-5790
(877) 798-9686
www.redfield.com
**Schmidt & Bender**
Am Grossacker 42
Biebertal
Hessen Germany 35444
011-49-6409-8115-0
www.schmidt-bender.de
**Shepherd Enterprises**
2920 North 240th St.
Waterloo, NE 68069
www.shepherdscopes.com
**Simmons**
9200 Cody
Overland Park, KS 66214-1734
(888) 276-5945
www.simmonsoptics.com
**Sightron Inc**
100 Jeffrey Way, Suite A
Youngsville, NC 27596
919-562-3000
www.sightron.com
**Swarovski Optik N. Amer.**
2 Slater Rd.
Cranston, RI 02920
401-734-1800
www.swarovskioptik.com
**Sift Instruments**
952 Dorchester Ave.
Boston, MA 02125
617-436-2960
www.swift-optics.com
**Thompson Center Com.**
P.O. Box 5002
Rochester, NH 03867
603-332-2394
www.tcarms.com
**Trijicon Inc**
49385 Shafer Ave.
Wixon, MI 48393
800-338-0563
www.trijicon.com
**TRUGLO Inc.**
13745 Neutron Rd.
Dallas, TX 75244
972-774-0300
www.truglo.com
**Ultra Dot**
6304 Riverside Dr.
Yankeetown, FL 34498-0362
352-447-2255
www.ultradotusa.com
**U.S. Optics Technologies**
5900 Dale St.
Buena Park, CA 90621
714-994-4901
www.usoptics.com
**Weaver Optics**
Weaver Optics
Onalaska Operations
N5549 County Trunk Z
Onalaska, WI 54650
(800) 635-7656
www.weaveroptics.com
**Williams Gun Sight**
7389 Lapeer Rd.
Davison, MI 48423
800-530-9028
www.williamsgunsight.com
**Carl Zeiss Optics**
13005 N. Kingston Av.
Chester, VA 23836
800 441-3005
www.zeiss.com

## MOUNTS, RINGS
**Aimtech Mount Systems**
P.O. Box 223
Thomasville, GA 31799-0223
229-226-4313

www.aimtech-mounts.com
**B-Square**
2708 Saint Louis Ave.
Fort Worth, TX 76110
800-433-2909
www.b-square.com
**Burris Company**
331 East 8th St.
Greeley, CO 80631-9559
970-356-1670
www.burrisoptics.com
**Custom Quality Mounts**
345 West Girard St.
Madison Heights, MI 48071
248-585-1616
**Kwik-Site Company**
5555 Treadwell
Wayne, MI 48184
734-326-1500
www.kwiksitecorp.com
**Leupold & Stevens**
14400 NW Greenbriar Pkwy.
Beaverton, OR 97006
503-646-9171
www.leupold.com
**Millett Sights**
16131-K Gothard St.
Huntington Beach CA 92647
714-842-5575
www.millettsights.com
**Redfield Mounts**
P.O. Box 39
Onalaska, WI 54650
800-635-7656
www.redfield-mounts.com
**Simmons Mounts**
P.O. Box 39
Onalaska, WI 54650
800-635-7656
www.simmons-mounts.com
**Stoney Point Products**
1822 N. Minnesota St.
New Ulm, MN 56073-0234
507-354-3360
www.stoneypoint.com
**Talley Manufacturing**
P.O. Box 821
Glenrock, WY 82637
307-436-8724
www.talleyrings.com
**Warne Scope Mounts**
9057 SE Jannsen Rd.
Clackamas, OR 97015
503-657-5590
www.warnescopemounts.com
**Weaver**
P.O. Box 39
Onalaska, WI 54650
800-635-7656
www.weaver-mounts.com
**Wideview Scope Mounts**
13535 S. Highway 16
Rapid City, SD 57702
605-341

# Index